Raymond Berry's

Complete Guide to

Coaching Pass Receivers

Raymond Berry with
C.H. "Butch" Gilbert, Jr.

Parker Publishing Co., Inc.   West Nyack, New York

© 1982, by

PARKER PUBLISHING COMPANY, INC.

West Nyack, N.Y.

Library of Congress Cataloging in Publication Data

Berry, Raymond.
    Raymond Berry's complete guide to coaching
pass receivers.

    Includes index.
    1. Passing (Football)   2. Football coaching.
I. Gilbert, C.H.   II. Title.
III. Title: Complete guide to coaching pass
receivers.
GV951.5.B47   796.332'25   82-2140
ISBN   0-13-753210-5   AACR2

About the Authors

RAYMOND BERRY played split end for the Baltimore Colts from 1955 to 1967. During his 13 NFL seasons he caught 631 passes for 9,275 yards and a 14.7 yards per catch average, placing him third on the all-time list of receivers.

For three straight years—1958, '59, and '60—he led the NFL in receptions, combining with quarterback Johnny Unitas for one of the most successful passing combinations in the history of the game.

A Hall of Fame inductee in 1973, Mr. Berry has coached at the University of Arkansas on the collegiate level, and for the Dallas Cowboys, Detroit Lions, Cleveland Browns, and New England Patriots in the professional ranks.

C.H. "BUTCH" GILBERT, JR. is presently a high school principal at West Elk Junior-Senior High School in Howard, Kansas. He was formerly Head Football Coach at F.L. Schlagle High School in Kansas City.

What This Book
Will Do for You

Despite all the offensive and defensive innovations over the years, the forward pass is still one of the most exciting phases of the game of football on any level. The forward pass ranks alongside the kicking game as an area that, in a single play, can turn a team around and change the outcome of a contest.

Talent is not always the prime factor in a successful passing attack. A receiver who runs exact, crisp routes, one who has closely coordinated his timing with that of the quarterback's, and one who knows how to catch the football, has the basics of any passing offense. The other basics necessary to the receiver are: a quarterback who can pass, and sufficient protection to give the quarterback time to throw.

Receivers are not always born, but they can be made with hard work—patterns run until they are second nature and footballs caught at every opportunity before, during, and after practices. A receiver has to have some natural talent, but by proper practice he can vastly improve his talents and become very productive.

The forward pass is not only exciting, it is an essential fundamental, the mastery of which often separates winners from losers. Whether a team passes with frequency or not, a completion is the desired result whenever the football is put into the air.

This book provides coaches with drills, individual routes and techniques, all of which can be incorporated into any offense to improve the passing game. Although primarily intended for coaching the receivers, this guide contains useful information for coaching the quarterback and all other football players in the areas of pre-season conditioning, prevention of injuries, increasing speed, and developing confident mental attitudes in players.

Much of the pass receiving information is divided into the areas of the wide receiver, the tight end, and the running back. The chapters pertaining to these three positions include every phase of receiving from stance and release to running with the ball and blocking. To enable quick reference within each chapter, material has been reiterated so that each chapter is complete.

As with any skill, mastery comes only with correct repetition. Chapter Two will enable your receivers to realize quick results within a minimum of time. Each drill is explained in detail complete with coaching points. These drills were refined by Raymond Berry when he was split end for the Baltimore Colts and have been used by him in his coaching of receivers on the college and professional levels. Regardless of how often a team passes, implementation of these drills will increase the skills of the receivers and improve the effectiveness of any pass offense.

All coaches and players want to be associated with a winning program. Each new season brings with it the striving to become a championship team. Even though nothing can guarantee victory, the probability of success can be increased by helping the individual player focus his attention on the thing that will result in his best contribution—realizing his full potential.

However large the role of the passing game to the total offensive scheme, these drills, patterns, and techniques can be utilized to make the passing game more effective and exciting for the coach, the players, and the fans.

Raymond Berry

Butch Gilbert

Acknowledgements

COACHES WHO HAVE INFLUENCED ME

I played for my dad the last two years in high school football. The perspective of the years has shown me that he was as fine a coach as I have ever been exposed to. I was influenced more by him than by any other person. He believed in simplicity, fundamentals, conditioning, balance and discipline, to name a few things. He never met an opponent he didn't believe his team could beat somehow—and his teams caught this belief from him.

My exposure to top coaches continued after leaving high school—Chena Gilstrap at Schreiner Junior College, Rusty Russell and Woody Woodard at SMU, and Weeb Ewbank and Don Shula at the Baltimore Colts.

My first experience in part-time coaching began while I was playing pro football. Coach Gilstrap had me work with his pass offense one spring. Then for several springs I worked with John Bridgers and Chuck Purvis at Baylor University.

As a professional player, my career was influenced more by Weeb Ewbank and Bob Shaw than any other coaches. Weeb saw something in me before anyone else did and gave me the chance to develop. Bob was an ex-pro receiver who was skilled at handling athletes and communicating his knowledge. His concepts of running routes opened a completely new perspective for me. Bob was a great teacher of the art of being a receiver.

As a coach, I have been greatly influenced by all the men already mentioned. In addition, Don Shula displayed his considerable talents as a coach my last five years as a player in Baltimore. I was privileged to work under Tom Landry in

Dallas for the first two years of my career as a full-time coach. I'm still drawing on all I was exposed to while on his staff.

I spent three years on Frank Broyles' staff at Arkansas; three years with the Detroit Lions under Don McAfferty, then Rick Forzano; two years with the Cleveland Browns and Forrest Gregg; and most recently with the New England Patriots, first with Chuck Fairbanks and then Ron Erhardt. From each of these men, along with members of their coaching staffs, I have gained valuable knowledge and insights.

R. B.

Table of Contents

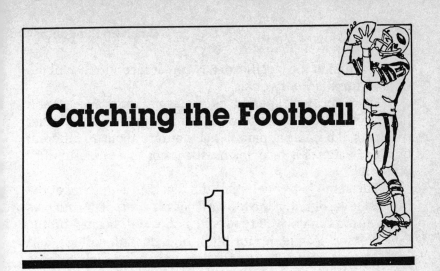

Catching the Football

1

WHY A RECEIVER MUST MASTER
A VARIETY OF CATCHES

On game day a pass receiver has four main responsibilities in the passing game: to get open, to catch the football, to run with it, and to maintain possession of the ball. It does little good to get open (and the receiver isn't going to run with the ball) if he doesn't catch it; and it does little good to catch the ball unless he is going to hang onto it when he gets hit or tackled.

This chapter deals primarily with the catching routine or program I learned and used while playing for the Baltimore Colts, and have been teaching to young athletes as a coach.

This routine of drills was the single most important thing I did in preparing for competition. Catching the football and avoiding fumbles is the number one responsibility of every receiver regardless of his individual talents. I used this routine during every practice and believe it to be instrumental in the fact that of 631 career receptions with the Colts, I fumbled only once.[1]

From my own experiences of trial and error, success and failure, and from observing the same experiences of other receivers, it became apparent that there are about 20 different types of catches a receiver must master to realize his full potential.

The same is true whether the receiver is playing at the highest level or not. If the forward pass is a part of the offense, these approximately 20 types of catches will occur—on the Pop Warner League, junior high, high school, college, and professional levels. It is impossible to know which of these catches will come up in the game at hand. For example, a receiver may go nearly a full season and never have a ball thrown high and behind him. Then it may happen twice in one game. The receiver never knows, but he has the responsibility of being ready. One thing I did learn is that if I had worked on a catch hard enough in practice then my chances of catching that type of pass in a game were greatly improved, and the odds went up in my favor.

HOW TO CATCH A LOT OF BALLS DURING PRACTICE

I discovered that I could get valuable training on these different catches without having to run full pass routes. This made it possible to catch an *additional 50 to 75 footballs per practice* without wearing my legs out. A receiver's legs have to be fresh and ready to go on game day. Since pass receiving is a skill, it is improved most by correct repetition, and

---

[1]There are two films available for purchase that illustrate the catching drills and pass routes described in this book. *There's a Catch to It*, a color, sound, 16mm film shows the catch in practice, then in an actual game. *Making the Moves* is a 16mm film series showing each move in practice situations, then in an actual game. For more information write: Raymond Berry Films, Box 285, Paris, Texas 75460.

catching an additional 50 to 75 footballs per practice enables receivers to realize the necessary repetition in less time.

This method requires a backdrop, preferably a net, for uncaught footballs. The backdrop is essential to save time which would otherwise be wasted shagging balls, but a fence or wall is too damaging to the footballs. Nets that fasten to practice goalposts to allow two groups of receivers to work simultaneously can be purchased or fashioned. The receiver positions himself in front of the backdrop as he would be positioned in a pass route. (To avoid letting your quarterbacks develop bad habits from throwing bad passes, have a coach or another receiver throw the desired type of passes.)

The receiver jogs lightly in place until the passer starts his throwing motion, then the receiver moves into the ball with a minimum of running. The passer fires the ball to a point designated by the drill while the receiver moves parallel to the net and catches the ball as in Figure 1-1.

Before sending receivers out onto the practice field you can list the catches or drills you want the receivers to work on. The object for each receiver is to go down the list, catching two or three of each type drill, and systematically expose himself to the football as much as possible. A list of the drills can be displayed on a sign permanently placed near the net. As the season progresses the list can be altered to reflect the different areas certain receivers need more work in. In addition, by utilizing odd moments during practice, for example, returning to the huddle, someone can be designated to fire the football at a receiver, thus enabling him to catch even more balls during a normal practice.

CORRECT REPETITION IS NECESSARY
FOR SKILL LEARNING

If there is not a special effort made to see to it that a receiver catches a lot of balls, he can go through a

NET

The catch should be made in front
of the middle of the net.

Figure 1-1

one-and-a-half to two-hour practice and catch only 5 to 10
passes. If this is all the work on catching he gets, then his
pass-catching ability will remain largely undeveloped and
untrained. His performance will be based almost entirely on
natural ability, and this means passes dropped that should
not be and stalled drives.

This was my experience when I first began to play pro
ball. Though I had what people referred to as "naturally good
hands," I was sometimes not able to catch a lot of passes that I
got my hands on. In later years I realized that though I had
good hands, they were not properly trained at that stage of
my development. The missing ingredient was the proper
amount of practice and repetition. I'm talking about 50 to 75
balls a day, 3 or 4 of each type of catch.

The principle involved is very similar to that used in
teaching typewriting to beginners. You start with hands that
have the ability to type, but simply haven't been trained. By
sticking to a disciplined, organized routine of drill, practice,
and repetition, a person gradually acquires the skill of
typing.

In order to have your receivers catch 50 to 75 passes a
day, you use two methods: First, have them catch what they
can from the quarterback while they are working on their

routes and the passing game during practice. After keeping statistics and records on this for several years I've found that this will usually amount to 5 to 10 catches on the average, and frequently less than that. (This may be hard to believe, but you can make a simple check yourself by just having someone follow a receiver all during practice and record each opportunity he has to catch a football.) Second, work on catching two, three, or four of each type of pass as described in Chapter Two. This second method requires a maximum amount of catching with a minimum amount of leg work. In 15 minutes a receiver can catch approximately 60 passes, three or four of each type.

In addition to developing a physical skill, another big effect of doing something successfully repeatedly, is the positive effect it has on the mental attitude. All receivers need confidence in order to catch the ball consistently under pressure. Proper practice and preparation are prime factors in developing confidence.

From my own experience, not only as a player but also as a coach, I know that any receiver willing to work and stick with this routine is going to increase his catching ability, gain confidence, and reduce dropped passes. The payoff is going to come in extra catches and one extra catch can mean the difference in a team's entire season. That is definitely worth working for.

HOW TO HOLD AND CARRY THE FOOTBALL

The number one fundamental is how to hold and carry the football. The nose of the ball should rest snugly in the fingers, which are spread over the point. The hand should have a tight grip on the nose of the ball. Pressure is put on the rear of the ball with the inside of the elbow and arm. The ball should be squeezed in toward the side. As the ball swings back and forth in the natural running rhythm, the receivers should learn to maintain this tight grip and pressure. As they get into heavy traffic they should be even more conscious of keeping the ball in close to their bodies, even covering it with the other arm and hand when they are trapped or surrounded.

Going through the motions physically in developing this habit has value, but if you encourage mental intensity along with the physical motions then the type of receivers that all coaches want will be developed—ones who won't fumble. Making your receivers determined to be this type of receiver pays off for them and for you. As I mentioned before, out of my 631 receptions as a professional I fumbled once. I am as proud of that one statistic as any other in my career.

FUNDAMENTALS OF CATCHING THE FOOTBALL

A receiver needs to concentrate on only two fundamentals of catching: the first is to watch the ball into the hands, and the second is to tuck it away quickly and tightly. Coach your receivers to do this every time they make a catch. Then see to it that they work on the different types of catches systematically through drill and repetition. Their natural style will develop and you will be keeping it simple. Emphasize just two things—watch it in and tuck it away. Coach your receivers to catch the ball naturally, which in most instances is the proper method anyway. Any style of catching is proper as long as the ball is caught!

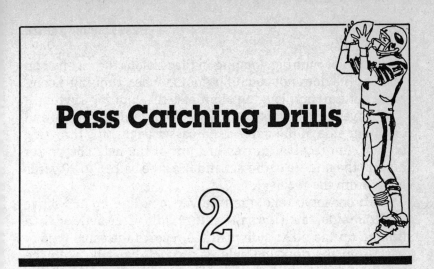

Pass Catching Drills

2

CATCHING THE SHORT PASS

The short pass is the bread and butter of the passing game. The biggest percentage of all passes caught are 15 yards or less. As the receiver makes his final cut, the ball is usually on the way. Characteristically, the short pass is thrown hard, with little trajectory, giving the receiver little time to react and adjust.

Drills for the short pass

High Look-In	Behind
High Back to the Passer	Back to the Passer
High Hook	One-Handed
High and Behind	Holler Ball
Low Ball	Concentration
Scoop	Toe Dance

THE SHORT PASSING DRILLS

The receiver doesn't have to do a lot of running on any of the short passing drills; just a few steps and catch. On most of the drills the receiver needs to jog very lightly in place until the passer starts his throwing motion. At the start of the throwing motion the receiver moves into the ball with a minimum of running. Jogging in place keeps the receiver on his toes (he does not catch flat-footed when running a complete pattern) and jogging simulates the running rhythm.

Have the receivers jog in place 4 to 5 yards in front of and on either side of the net. As the passer begins his throwing motion, the receiver moves in front of the net. The passer aims at the middle of the net and fires the ball 15 to 20 yards away from the receiver.

To conserve time, the receivers can line up and move from one side, catch the ball in the middle of the net, and then line up on the other side ready to receive the same type of pass from the opposite side. If a coach can't be with the receivers during these drills or if the coach wants two groups working simultaneously on both sides of the net, then the receivers can make the position of passer a stop in the rotation of the line. It is better not to use quarterbacks in these drills to avoid the possibility of their developing bad habits.

Everyone involved in the drill must keep moving quickly to have the maximum number of receptions attempted. Mentally, this is beneficial because the receivers are forced to concentrate fully on the drill for the entire time.

The "High Look-In" drill

This situation usually occurs when the receiver breaks inside on the "Look-In" or "Short Post" patterns. In this drill, have the receivers stand at the edge of the net and jog in place. Instruct the passer to fire the ball high and hard at the middle of the net. The receiver should move parallel to the net, leap, and make the catch. Emphasize only two things: watch the ball into the hands and put it away quickly and tightly. Let the receiver use his natural style of catching this type of pass (either thumbs in or thumbs out).

Generally, a receiver has a *dominant* hand, one in which he has better touch. In the process of catching, this dominant hand will often instinctively do the main part of stopping the ball while the other hand will support the dominant one. Experience plus work on the weaker hand in the "One-Handed" drill will help equalize the hands.

Coaching Points: Keep the receivers moving. At least three footballs are needed with a manager or someone available to feed balls to the passer. The passer fires as soon as he is ready to. After making the catch, the receivers clear the net, toss the ball to the feeder, and take up positions for the next drill. See Figure 2-1.

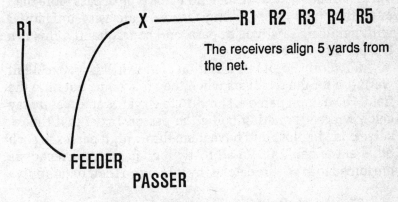

The receivers align 5 yards from the net.

The passer aligns 12 to 15 yards from the receivers.

Figure 2-1

The "High Back to the Passer" drill

The receiver positions himself in the middle of the net, 5 yards away from it, with his back to the passer. He jogs in place, turns his head to see the passer, who zips the ball in high and hard at a point high above the receivers ear or shoulder. The receiver should have to leap to catch the pass. Again, don't be concerned about hand position; the natural instincts are usually correct. The receiver must concentrate on keeping his eye on the ball. This drill is excellent for developing the timing and coordination necessary to make a leap from the running motion, therefore the receiver must be jogging in place on his toes.

Most receivers grow up learning to play catch the baseball way—throwing the ball back and forth while facing each other. Under game conditions, many of a receiver's catches put him in a position where he is looking back over his shoulder at the passer for short bullet passes and medium arch balls as well as for the deep pass. Back-to-the-passer situations come about primarily on the sideline routes, and also on post area routes where the ball is drilled as the receiver moves away from the passer. Tight ends and backs out of the backfield have to handle this type of pass more than any other type. Most young receivers are very unfamiliar with handling this type of pass, and consequently, this is a top priority drill.

Coaching Points: A variation of this drill is an excellent warm-up for the receivers when they first come out onto the field. Have them pair off, stand 15 to 20 yards apart, and play catch while alternating being the passer. Insist that the receivers jog in place and have them throw high passes to each other at the net. As with all really high passes, the receivers are forced to make the catches by relying on their hands only.

The "High Hook" drill

In this drill have the receiver stay 5 yards away from the net and face it. He should then take a step toward the net and turn quickly to face the passer. As the receiver makes his turn, the passer should fire the ball high and hard. The ball should be high enough to make the receiver jump his highest to catch it. As in most short passing drills, the passer should be from 15 to 20 yards away from the receiver.

Under game conditions, a key fundamental on the "Hook" or "Turn-In" route is the receiver's footwork immediately after he makes the turn to face the passer. His feet should be spread, knees bent, and his weight on the balls of his feet. His stance should resemble that of a baseball shortstop just prior to the pitch. While the receivers are working on the "High Hook" catching drills, they should also work on their footwork and stance.

Emphasize to receivers that sloppy and careless footwork on this route can cause many passes to be missed. By assuming a good football "ready" position they will be better able to react to a ball that is thrown behind them or way inside, too high, or too low. This is not possible if the receiver's knees are not bent, or if he is bouncing up and down and gets caught with both feet off of the ground, or if his legs are crossing as the ball is arriving. Whatever the reason, the receiver cannot react if he is not in a "ready" position.

Coaching Points: Make sure the passer keeps the ball high enough to challenge the receivers. Have him make it tough on the receivers; it will pay off in the pressure situations. The net will stop the overthrows and the receivers will gradually get better about timing their jumps. In game situations the quarterbacks will often throw the ball high to get it over the linebackers, and the receiver who can go up and get these types of passes adds another dimension to the pass offense.

The "High Behind" drill

At the net the receiver positions himself the way he did for the "High Back to the Passer" drill. He jogs in place and looks back over his shoulder at the passer. In this drill, however, the passer will fire the ball in really high, but to the opposite side that the receiver is facing. Without losing sight of the ball, the receiver must turn and leap in the direction opposite to where his momentum is taking him and make the catch.

A receiver who can make this catch consistently will bring the fans to their feet quite a few times. He must not only time his jump to reach the high ball, but before that, he must stop and turn as soon as he sees the ball will be behind him. It takes some quick reactions and flawless footwork, plus timing and good hands. Without practicing this particular type of catch, this is one completion that might not have been.

Every receiver is troubled by some pass or passes that seem to be more of a challenge than others. This "High Behind" catch was the one for me. I worked on it for years. When it came up in a game it was always on the "Sideline" route. Sometimes I made the catch, and sometimes I didn't.

When I didn't, it was back to the net the following week for
more work. Practice will not guarantee 100% success, but the
receivers should understand that you are just trying to increase the odds in their favor.

The "Low Ball" drill

Catching the low pass can make the receiver feel awk-
ward. It is hard for him to keep his balance. Running forward,
bending over, stretching out his arms and reaching for a ball
throws his weight further forward. I usually ended up diving
and falling in a game, though this did not happen in practice.
Some receivers can reach down and catch a really low pass
and hardly break a stride. This is the type of receiver every
coach would like to have. Using the "Low Ball" drill daily
can help develop them.

Position the receiver a couple of yards outside the edge
of the net, keeping him 5 yards away from it. Have him jog in
place. As the passer starts his windup, the receiver should
start moving parallel across the front of the net. The passer
should place the ball low and out in front of the receiver. The
catch should be made near the center of the net.

Catches made by the various NFL receivers vary a great
deal. Some catches are pure hands (the extremely high ones),
and some are a combination of hands, forearms and wrists,
and body. My philosophy is that a receiver should use the
method that gets the best results for him, because I've seen
different receivers succeed using not only their hands in
catching, but also using their bodies in combination with
their hands. My personal experience is this: no matter how
much I worked on a particular catch using hands only, sometimes in a game situation instinct took over and I would go
for the ball using a combination of hands and also catching it
against my body. Finally, I just worked on both techniques,
realizing I might react to do either in the heat of the game. I
dropped passes both ways and I caught passes both ways, as
do most receivers.

I very seldom ever mention to receivers *how* to catch the ball. The thing I believe in most strongly is just make sure the receiver catches at least 50 balls a day, some of each kind of drill. He is forced to train his catching ability—the repetition brings out his natural style. In the meantime, all he really has to concentrate on is watching it in and tucking it away.

The "Scoop" drill

In my second year with the Colts, in a game with the 49ers, I ran a "Hook" or "Curl" route. John Unitas drilled the ball low into the open lane between the linebackers. I was set and waiting for the ball, watched it all the way, reached down to catch it, and it was gone. It was very low, but I had my hands on it. It went right between my legs. I couldn't figure out what happened to it until I watched the game film. When the ball had struck my hands it didn't stick but went right on through the opening between my elbows. This and similar experiences with very low passes taught me that I couldn't reach down and catch those type passes with my hands only. After that I started working on the "Scoop" technique. It paid off many, many times in games—not only on low balls over the middle, but also when fielding low passes on the sideline.

The purpose of the "Scoop" is to put a catching surface of hands, wrists, and forearms in front of the ball in order to keep the ball from getting through if it starts to rebound off of the hands. The receiver should work on closing the elbows. Then the ball will rebound upward into the stomach or chest. The "Scoop" technique acts to elevate a ball thrown inches off of the ground.

In front of the net, position the receiver in a "Hook" stance and also in the "Out" position. Have the passer drill the ball just off of the ground, only inches high. Since this pass is very difficult to throw, the passer may have to attempt several in order to get one to work for the receiver. One reason I'm sold on the "Jugs" passing machine is because it places the ball with flawless accuracy and velocity on all of these drills, and thus saves time. Very few high school programs are able to afford such expensive equipment, but if possible, purchasing a "Jugs" machine would provide precise placement of the football to work on the kicking game as well as the passing and defensive secondary phases of football.

The "Behind" drill

One of the toughest catches to make is the ball thrown behind the receiver, especially if he is moving at full speed. There are times when the quarterback may have to throw a pass behind the receiver due to the position of the defenders.

To work on this catch at the net requires very little running. Have the receivers jog slowly back and forth in front of the net and have the passer throw behind them at varying heights and distances.

These drills are not intended to aid conditioning of your receivers; they are intended to supplement the catching practice they get while running their routes with the quarterbacks. The point is that receivers can only do so much running per day and then they have to quit. But they can still do a lot of catching the ball without much leg work, which will be very valuable to your receivers.

The "Back to the Passer" drill

In this drill have the receiver face the net and jog in place while looking back over his shoulder at the passer. Instruct the passer to throw each receiver three balls on each side—ankle high, knee high, and shoulder high. This is one of the most important drills because so few receivers have really worked much at catching from this angle. Tight ends and backs especially must master this catch. Split receivers catch sideline passes from this angle as well.

Tell the passer to throw the ball hard and on a line. In most cases this will be a thumbs-out catch, but again, catching the ball is the object. This is usually a pure hands catch since the ball comes in over the shoulder or to the side at such an angle that the receiver cannot use his body to act as a backdrop. This drill really helps receivers develop good hands.

To make it easier on himself, the receiver will usually have a tendency to start turning his body sideways to the passer during this drill. Insist that he face the net and turn his head only.

The "One-Hand" drill

Occasionally a receiver can get only one hand on the ball. When this happens, and a receiver loses a long gain and possible touchdown, the "One-Hand" practice becomes much more meaningful for him. When he is out there on the practice field the next week he has a much clearer picture in his mind of what he is working to get better at and what he is working to prevent. Utilization of this drill should help receivers learn the lesson without the necessity of losing the long reception and the possible score.

There were two reasons why I started working on catching the ball with one hand. One was to help me improve my ability to make catches as described above. The other was to improve a weak left hand. My left hand had very poor touch when I first began to play pro ball. It showed up when I broke inside from my left end position. A ball out in front of me caused me to put my left hand out in front to do the main job of controlling the ball. I bobbled a lot of them, so I began to work on catching a lot of balls with my left hand only, in an attempt to improve it. The ball would strike my wrist, my palm, the side of my hand, but seldom would it hit in the web of the fingers. Catching with the "One-Hand" drill using my right hand was completely different. The ball would usually hit right into the fingers and there would be some give. All I would get with my left hand was a loud "splat." Over a period of time, however, the left hand began to develop better touch until it could handle a ball almost as well as my right hand.

The "Toe Dance" drill

Teaching receivers to develop the technique of dropping a foot inside the boundaries can pay off in first downs, and in the end zone. The receiver can develop a "feel" for knowing when to drop his foot inbounds. He doesn't take his eyes off of the ball, but he senses when it's going to be close. Once he's got the ball in his hands, he should try to drop one foot inside the boundary. He can make the decision easy for the official by clearly placing his foot well inside the line.

Many catches near the sidelines are made as the receiver is falling or diving over the boundary. The receiver should attempt to make his first contact with the ground with his feet so they drag across the sideline. When working on this technique it's best to work near a chalk line so that the receiver can work on the "feel" for the boundary while concentrating on the ball.

Early in the season this drill can be done in front of the net using a folded towel for the sideline. This drill, as well as the "Scoop" drill, is valuable in teaching receivers to go to the ground to make a catch. This is as important as diving for a loose basketball on the basketball floor. With these two drills receivers can learn the proper techniques to make a catch while diving, without risk of injury. Big gymnastic mats on the field could be used to teach receivers to dive for balls without injuring themselves.

The "Holler Ball" drill

We were playing the Bears in Chicago and I was running a sideline pattern. As I broke toward the outside I whipped my head around to pick up the ball. It was just a few yards from me. It startled me and I missed it. This made me realize that it is a lot easier to catch a ball if you get to see the passer release it and have the opportunity to watch it throughout its flight. However, if you get to watch it for only a short distance it makes for a much more difficult catch.

The purpose of the "Holler Ball" drill is to train the receiver's eyes and reflexes to make this quick reaction. This drill is also a very good one for your defensive players. If they are going to make an interception they usually only get to see the ball part way since they are intent upon the coverage of the receiver.

The receiver faces the net. He then raises either his right or left hand to indicate to the passer which side he should throw to. An instant before releasing the ball, the passer hollers, "Ball!" The receiver then turns quickly around. When he completes the turn with his body, he should be in a good football position and make the catch.

Receivers should wear their helmets in all drills, but in this one especially.

Coaching Points: Emphasize to the receivers that they should turn their heads quickly enough to pick up the flight of the ball before their bodies get turned around. They should be in a crouched, rather than an erect stance, before and after making the turn. They should get their shoulders around and squared to the passer before the ball arrives so that they are able to move in any direction to go get the ball.

The "Concentration" drill

This drill gets the receivers used to contact—being hit and knocked around while catching the ball. Have the harassing player mix up his tactics—bump the receiver from one side, then from the other side; get behind him and bump him high and then low; get out in front of him at least 5 yards and tip or deflect the ball and the next time just wave a hand across the flight of the ball without touching it. There are many ways of setting up gamelike distractions.

The receiver can use varied positions, ranging from facing the passer, to turning sideways, to back to the passer. It usually takes a few weeks to really keep his concentration in a crowd, but this will develop if he keeps on working on it—and it will pay off.

Lenny Lyles was the Colt defensive back whom I played against every day in practice. I used to ask Lenny to knock me around as I was catching the ball. It helped me get in the

groove. A defensive teammate can hit a receiver pretty well if
he uses good judgment and doesn't drive him into the
ground and fall on him or cut his legs out from under him.
Both of them will benefit and no one will get hurt in the
process.

As coach, you can control the amount of contact by
putting definite limits on what the harassing man can do.
Especially early in the season, maintain control in this area
until you feel the receivers are ready.

CATCHING THE LONG PASS

Coaching young receivers confirmed what I experienced myself: catching the long ball is the most advanced
part of the receiver's art.

There's nothing quite like catching the deep pass. It is a
great thrill. One reason is that the opportunities to catch this
type of pass are few, and a receiver may get one opportunity a
game at most. Another reason is that the payoff to catching
the long pass is always big yardage and possibly a
touchdown.

Working on timing with the passer, and developing the
concentration and skill necessary to catch the long pass can
get discouraging. I remember that without exception we
used to go through this every year. We would start working
on it and John would overthrow, underthrow, put it too far to
the outside, too far inside. Then he would throw it perfectly
and we would drop it. We knew we had to have the deep
pass, and we kept working on it day by day, week by week. As
always, it would start to come. But if we had let a little
discouragement stop us, we would never have gotten it
timed and working.

You must remain positive and encourage your receivers
in practice because the long ball timing is especially difficult
for young receivers to attain. Since a receiver doesn't get
many chances at the long ball, he really wants to cash in. He
will want to invest a lot of time and practice to prepare

himself for that one opportunity a game. When he does come up with the catch, it is worth it.

The consistent execution of the deep pass—both throwing it and catching it—is an absolute necessity if you are going to have a passing attack. But my experience is that it doesn't come easy and your receivers are going to have to stick with it.

FUNDAMENTALS OF CATCHING THE LONG BALL

The number one fundamental to learn is to maintain concentration on the ball. The receiver must keep his eye on the ball all the way into his hands. The tendency is to lose sight of it just before it reaches the hands, the last few inches. Most deep passes that are missed, are missed because of this break in concentration.

The second fundamental is speed. The tendency is for most young receivers to lose speed (consequently inches, and this is a game of inches) while turning the head to locate the ball. The receiver must practice maintaining top speed as he looks back for the ball. Learning to run smoothly while looking back and adjusting to get under the ball is a skill that one can develop by the proper work. Ideally, the receiver should be just like the sprinter moving down the track. The act of turning his head to look back for the ball should have a minimum effect on his running form. He should turn his head only and not twist his entire upper body around. The more he twists, the more his speed will be affected.

The rule is for the receiver to come off the breaking point (after he has completed his move) with speed. He should turn on the speed as he races for the ball and as he looks back he should maintain top speed. If making the catch causes him to lose speed (as is usually the case unless it's an absolutely perfect pass) he should strive again for top speed after the ball is safely tucked away.

HOW TO DEVELOP SKILL
IN CATCHING THE LONG BALL

In order to get the timing down on catching the long pass, it is necessary to run many, many of these routes at full speed so the receivers get used to watching the ball while moving at top speed, and adjusting to the ball as it comes in—sometimes over the inside shoulder, sometimes over the outside shoulder, and sometimes directly overhead. This involves a 50- to 60-yard sprint (including the distance covered after the receiver tucks the ball away and attains full speed) and there is a limit to how many of these sprints receivers can run every day.

In addition to catching balls while running the entire route, receivers can get a lot of value out of doing just the last few yards. As in the short drills, these long pass drills are intended to be in *addition to* the regular work with the quarterback. The object is a maximum of catching and a minimum of running to sharpen the catching skills.

Drills for the deep pass

Inside Shoulder

Directly Overhead

Deep Outside Shoulder

End Line Toe Dance

Tightrope Toe Dance

Wrong Shoulder

Harassment

The receiver can work on the "Inside Shoulder" drill, the "Directly Overhead" drill, and the "Deep Outside Shoulder" drill all at one time. He should position himself about 25 yards downfield with his back to the passer. The passer should arch the ball high and long and 10 yards directly in front of the receiver's head. Once the passer learns to throw these drills, the receiver should not have to move much beyond 10 yards to make the catch. These drills should be timed so that the ball drops over the receiver's head or his shoulder and he should make the catch with his arms out-stretched. (The receiver should be positioned downfield with his head turned to look back at the passer and he should not start moving downfield until the passer has released the ball.) Even though the receivers are doing only the tail end of the deep ball on all of these drills, they should still be any-where from 25 to 35 yards away from the passer each time they catch the ball, to simulate actual game conditions.

After looking over his right shoulder awhile, the re-ceiver should turn and look over his left shoulder and have the passer repeat the throws. In the process of catching 10 to 15 balls he will get some of each of the three types of passes.

Coaching Points: When a receiver looks back for the ball on a "Deep Post" route, only a slight turn of the head is required usually. This is the easiest vision situation on the deep ball. When he breaks to the deep outside on the "Flag" or "Corner" routes he is faced with a much tougher problem. Here he is required to really turn his head quite a bit in order to locate the ball. Have your receivers try to do this without twisting their bodies too much, so they don't slow them-selves down. They should practice and concentrate on turn-ing the head only and not the upper body, while at the same time running at full speed.

Another mistake that will cost receivers a step is extend-ing the hands and arms for the ball too soon. Ideally, the receiver should maintain top speed (assuming the ball doesn't slow him down by being underthrown) as the ball comes into him. He should stick out his hands to make the catch just as the ball gets there. If he extends them too soon, which is the tendency with an inexperienced receiver, he will run along a few steps with his arms stuck out and this will throw him off balance and slow him down.

The "End Line Toe Dance" drill

The first time I became aware of this type of catch was when one of our flankers made a nice catch deep in the end

zone, but lost a touchdown when he failed to keep his feet
inside the back edge of the end zone. It had never occurred to
me until then that there would be a need to use the toe dance
technique on the long pass. After that we started working on
dropping our feet after catching the long ball over the shoulder so we would react properly if it ever happened again.

It did happen—several times—and the training paid off.
On this drill the payoff is always a touchdown.

The receivers work on this drill the same way they did
on the "Inside Shoulder" drill. Have them stand on the goal
line and instruct the passer to arch the ball so it is caught
directly on the end line—still having the ball travel 25 to 35
yards in the air. The passer should throw over the receiver's
inside shoulder, outside shoulder, and directly over his head
as well.

The "Tightrope Toe Dance" drill

The use of this drill's technique occurs when the receiver is racing deep on an "Up" route and he is fairly close to
the sideline. For example, he may be split out to the left side,
with the ball on the left hash mark, and that puts him into the
short side of the field. He puts his move on the defender and
takes off deep. The quarterback puts the ball into the air and
as it drops into him it becomes necessary to lean out over the
boundary line to make the catch while still keeping his feet
inside the boundary. Frequently, just after such a catch his
body momentum will take him completely out of bounds.
This is a unique type of toe dance technique which occurs
often.

To duplicate this in practice takes a little skill and accuracy on the part of the passer. The way I throw this drill to my
receivers is to get them about 4 or 5 yards from the sideline
and 20 to 25 yards downfield from me. I will stand almost on
the near hash mark and arch the ball over their heads and in
front of them. When I throw it accurately, they should catch it
as they are leaning over the sideline, while keeping their feet
inbounds. Long gains and touchdowns are the payoffs to this
drill.

The "Wrong Shoulder" drill

This situation is one that will occur a couple of times a year. A receiver may be expecting the ball over his outside shoulder on a "Deep Corner" or "Flag" route, but the ball is thrown further downfield, forcing him to turn and re-adjust under it, making it an inside shoulder catch. Or, the receiver may be expecting the ball over the inside shoulder such as on a "Post" route and the ball is thrown in such a way that he is forced to turn and catch it over his head or over his outside shoulder.

The ability to make this adjustment is worth it. This drill will help your receivers learn to turn from one side to the other, (taking their eyes off of the ball as they change direction) pick up the flight of the ball again quickly, and sprint to it. Another value is that they learn to judge the flight of the ball when it is only a short distance from them. This is a good drill for defensive backs to work on as well.

This drill is especially valuable in light of the fact that modern quarterbacks are being coached to throw the ball into the open area even if it is not directly in line with the receiver's route. The theory behind this is that if the ball is thrown into the open area it will not be intercepted and the receiver can break off his route or adjust it to make the catch. Not every route will need to be adjusted, but secondary coverages will dictate that some passes will have to be thrown to the open areas. The odds favoring a completion will increase with the utilization of this drill.

When the receiver sees that he is going to have to turn, lose sight of the ball for a moment, and then go after it, he must remember to whip his head around quickly and maintain top speed during his change of direction.

To practice this drill, position the receiver 20 to 25 yards downfield of the passer. The receiver should indicate which shoulder he is going to look back over by raising that arm. Then he starts moving while looking over that shoulder. The passer will then arch the ball over the other shoulder. The receiver must go and get it. Have the receivers catch three on one side then repeat the drill on the other side.

The "Harassment" drill

Frequently on the long pass the receiver will be racing downfield and the ball will be underthrown a little. He has to put on the brakes while keeping his eyes on the ball and then go up and get it. Most of the time the defender is right there with him, also leaping for the ball. The purpose of this drill is to train the receiver to react—stop, jump, watch it in—while at the same time not letting the defender distract him. Another guy going for the ball at the same time makes it much more difficult to concentrate on the pass and to maintain balance when jumping.

Pair the receivers off with one another and have them get 25 to 30 yards away from the passer. Have the passer arch the ball into the area. I recommend that you designate one player to harass, the other to catch—especially with young receivers or early in the season. (It is more risky if both receivers are fighting for the ball, though it is a better game simulation.) The harassing player just watches the one who is catching, and when the ball is thrown, he jars him, slaps him on the helmet, distracts him, etc. The receiver concentrates on watching the ball and trying to go up and get it at the highest point. After the receiver catches three or four balls, they switch positions and he becomes the harasser.

This was for me the toughest deep ball situation. The reaction just would not come unless I really drilled on it. On several occasions when this situation came up in a game and I had not been working on it, I looked up at the ball, and the next thing I knew I was on my back. On other occasions, when I had been working on this drill in practice, the reactions just came automatically.

UTILIZATION OF THIS DRILL ROUTINE

This is a routine any receiver can do and one that any receiver will benefit from. If he works for 15 minutes a day and catches three of each type of pass, he will catch 60 balls;

in a 10-minute drill period catching two of each type, 40 balls; and in 5 minutes catching one of each type, 20 balls.

MOTIVATION FOR RECEIVERS

This routine is for the player who is not satisfied and who wants to improve his pass-catching skills and is willing to work to do so. He should expect to improve. You, as his coach, should expect him to improve and he should be aware of your expectations. If he sticks to this routine, he will improve noticeably in a few weeks.

This will require self-discipline on his part and will result in his being prepared for game situations. When the chips are down, this discipline and preparation will pay off. The receiver's extra work will result in extra catches.

Coaches can do much to hasten this improvement by making sure that the drills are run correctly by each receiver, insisting that attention be paid to detail. Another method to aid this improvement and build confidence in your receivers is to see to it that each drill is geared to the receivers' success in those drills. For example, early in the season the passer should take a little off of the ball until the receivers are familiar with the drills and until they are capable of handling the harder, more difficult passes. It is also asking a great deal of a receiver who is inexperienced to have the same degree of success in catching the hard, difficult throws as the more experienced and talented receivers. If your young receivers aren't allowed to succeed also, they will be hard pressed to come up with the concentration and self-discipline necessary to improve.

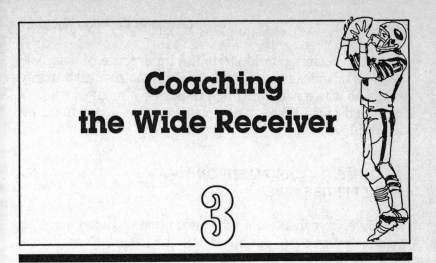

Coaching the Wide Receiver

3

CHARACTERISTICS OF THE POSITION

The wide receiver position is unique. No other position has caused defenses to adjust so many ways to contain it. The zone defense, rotations, double coverages, combinations, bump and run, are all methods to counter the wide receiver.

From his position (the wide receiver is usually lined up across from the quickest defenders), the wide receiver is usually able to release from the line with relative ease, is in a position to see what the quarterback sees as the defense moves on the snap, and is able to make the defense react to him in some manner. Even on a running play, the defensive secondary initially reacts in part to the wide receiver.

When not in a pattern, a great deal of the time the wide receiver is a decoy. When he is required to block, it is usually a severe angle block such as a crack back or a downfield block or a stalk block when he delays and then attacks the defender as the ball carrier approaches. A good wide receiver cannot afford to perform poorly at any of these assignments. Even though receiving is stressed, all receivers should be aware of the necessity of being capable at all phases of their position in order to be successful, complete receivers.

All coaches should stress the importance of complete receivers. No team can afford a player who goes all out only when he is in a pattern, which is usually a small percentage of actual game time. A complete receiver gives 100% on every play.

ALIGNMENT—CAPITALIZE ON WHAT
THE DEFENSE GIVES

Every receiver should be aware that no defense can be strong against every option open to the offense. Every defensive alignment will give up something in order to be in a position to stop something else. That knowledge, combined with an understanding of the offense and what each play is designed to do, should be at the command of every receiver as he lines up.

If a receiver consistently lines up 6 yards from the next man on the line of scrimmage regardless of the play, he is making things easier on the defense. If however, he varies his alignment a little from play to play, he can create wider holes at the point of attack. For example, instead of lining up 6 yards wide for an off-tackle play, the split end aligns 8 yards wide and draws the defensive cornerback out with him. The cornerback cannot support the off-tackle hole from the outside nearly as well from 8 yards as he could from 6 yards. On a passing play, if the wide receiver will align wider, as the field permits, he will stretch the secondary whether it is playing man-to-man or zone coverage. This stretch will put additional pressure on the outside men as well as the linebackers who have responsibility for the underneath coverage as well as for the run.

As the receiver lines up he should recognize the way the defensive back is playing him at the same time the quarterback recognizes it. Both should realize when the ball will have to be delivered for the pattern to be successful. This, in other words, is taking what the defense is giving. Anything the offense can do to unsettle the defense is beneficial.

STANCE—THE BALANCED BEGINNING OF EVERY SUCCESSFUL PATTERN

Most receivers get down in a sprinter's stance, or the three-point stance. I would recommend this stance for your split receivers. It is helpful if they always have their inside foot back when they are split out. This will help them in their execution of blocking assignments later on. Ideally, if you have your receivers flip-flop, this will help them run consistent routes. In other words, on the left side the right foot should be back and the right hand down, while on the right side the left foot should be back and the left hand down.

Some receivers in the wide receiver positions prefer an upright or standing stance. Although it gives good vision of the defense, the drawback is that the receiver has trouble exploding off of the line of scrimmage, which gives the defender additional time to read his keys and react to them.

RELEASING—BREAKING CLEANLY OFF OF THE LINE INTO THE ROUTE

If the defense assigns a man to delay your wide receivers from getting off the line, your receivers will need some quick fakes to escape. Quickness is vital, so the receiver must explode on the snap count. The release fakes shown in Figure 3-1 are for a receiver on the left side. By practice and repetition a receiver can develop these to the degree that he can execute them quickly and still maintain good balance. Stress to your receivers that if a defender walks right up onto their nose that they have to even up their stance—get both feet even or nearly so—to allow movement quickly either in or out.

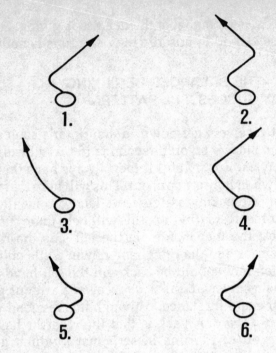

Shown for a receiver on the left side.

1. Make one step outside with the outside foot. Be low and quick going inside.

2. Make one step out with the outside foot, then one quick step inside with the inside foot. A real quick "one-two," then go outside.

3. Flare release. Stay low. Make the first step with the inside foot, crossing it over, then the second step with the outside foot.

4. Fake flare, release inside. Crossover with the right, up with the left and plant to go back inside.

5. Hop inside, release outside.

6. Hop outside, release inside. Stay low.

Figure 3-1

Six Methods of Releasing

WIDE RECEIVER PATTERNS— MAKING THE MOVES

The "Quick Out"

Purpose of the Route: To attack the short flat area. The defense is not covering it with linebackers and the defensive halfback is not tight enough to stop it.

Alignment: To the short side of the field. Have the receiver at least 8 yards from the sideline. If the ball is in the middle of the field, align him 11 yards from the sideline. If the receiver is split to the wide side of the field, have him align on the hash mark or a little inside it. These splits should give your quarterback help. If his arm isn't too strong, move the receivers in to accommodate the passer's arm.

Approach: The receiver should explode off of the line and drive to the defender's outside shoulder or right at him. (If he's really loose it may not make any difference.) If the receiver is going to widen to the outside on his approach, he should keep this in mind when he lines up. For instance, on the short side of the field if the receiver is to widen a yard, he should line up 9 yards from the sideline to avoid running out of field.

Steps: We ran this route at Baltimore using a three-step move. For example, a wide receiver on the left side starts with the inside foot back—right, left, right and breaks to the outside, rounding into the break. If a player is a short, quick strider he could take three long steps and two quick, short, gathering steps—right, left, right—left, right and break to the outside sharply as in Figure 3-2. It will time out the same. Caution receivers against being in a hurry and shortening their strides or breaking too early. Both of these tendencies disrupt the timing. The time lapse from the explosion off of the line to the break should be about 1.4 seconds. Exact timing will be established only after many, many repetitions between the quarterback and the receiver.

Coaching Point: Shortly after introduction of this route, receivers need to be coached to turn upfield—to explode

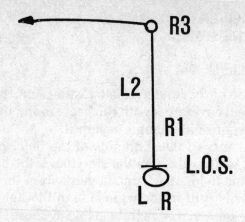

All of these moves (refer to moves shown in Figures 3-2 through 3-10) are shown for a receiver lined up on the left side, with his inside foot (right foot) back in his stance before the ball is snapped.

The circles on the diagram indicate where a "break" is made—a change of direction, a pivot, a planting of the foot.

Once the final break is made no steps are numbered or shown. It is understood that the "move" is over once the final break is made. From that point, turn on the speed! Explode! Run! The only exception to this is on curl or hook routes, and some inside routes where the receiver does control his speed to a degree when working against zone defenses. In this case he throttles his speed when in open seams of the zone, between the defenders.

Figure 3-2

The Quick Out

upfield—if for any reason the timing is thrown off before the quarterback can deliver the ball. This pattern will not be effective if the receiver slows down, stops his route, or continues to the point that he makes the catch out of bounds. When the receiver turns his head around to look for the ball, if the pass hasn't been thrown, then he should plant his outside foot and explode as hard as he can upfield. This route then becomes the "Quick Out and Up," as shown in Figure 3-3.

Whenever the timing is disrupted in practice or in a game this should be an automatic adjustment. Your quarterback may stumble before he can set up, he may have to sidestep a defender, or he may just be slow on occasion. When something like this happens, the quarterback and the receiver should both adjust, thereby salvaging an opportunity for a pass completion.

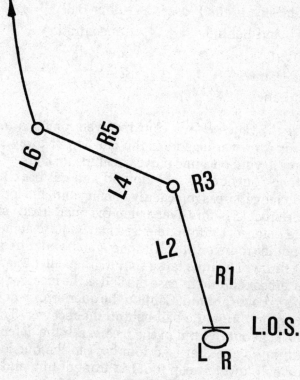

Figure 3-3

The Quick Out and Up

Breaking Point: The receiver should explode off the approach to the outside with speed, especially if he is run-

ning from the middle or the wide side of the field. The passer
will more than likely put the ball out in front of the receiver,
who should anticipate this and be running at full speed. He
should do the same on the short side of the field as well. I've
missed completions on this route on the short side by failing
to run at full speed.

The Catch: Emphasize watching the ball all the way into
the hands and tucking it away quickly and tightly. Catching
drills that help prepare for this route are

High Back to the Passer	Holler Ball
High and Behind	Concentration
Behind	Low Ball
One Hand	Scoop
Toe Dance	

After the Catch: Have your receivers practice turning
upfield for extra yardage after the ball is put away safely.
They should work on some moves to elude tacklers—fake in
and get back outside, or fake upfield and cut back inside.
With each move, stress repeatedly to hang onto the football.

Quarterback: Before every snap the quarterback should
check the defense. Certain defenses may require an audible
call to another route or play. Dropback steps are three steps
back and throw. The time lapse should be about 1.5 seconds.
The quarterback should release the ball as the receiver's head
is starting to come around. Caution the quarterback not to be
late and not to throw the ball behind the receiver. The ball
should be kept out in front of the receiver. If the defender is
tight on him, then either lead him back to the outside and
throw the ball low, or keep it out in front of him and high.
This will avoid the interception.

The "Quick Out and Up"

Purpose of the Route: To take advantage of a defender
who is trying to break up or intercept the "Quick Out." This

move is most effective and has its best chance of working when the halfback is tight; when he doesn't have a sufficient "cushion." When the receiver breaks to the outside, the defender is within 1 to 2 or maybe 3 yards of the receiver and reacting hard. The key is that the receiver is able to turn upfield after the out fake and get by his defender and also avoid running into him. If he has too much of a cushion, it is easy for him to recover and bump the receiver.

Alignment: This is a move that requires some room so the distance the receiver splits is very important. It helps to have the receiver split to the wide side of the field. If he is split to the wide side with the ball on the hash mark, have him align on the other hash mark. If the ball is in the middle, have him allow at least 11 yards between himself and the sideline. If the ball is on a hash and the receiver is split to the short side of the field, the "Quick Out and Up" is not a very good risk. The receiver is too restricted by the boundary. He should be aware that from the time he leaves the LOS, makes his outside move, and turns upfield, he will have widened nearly 10 yards. This route will also require 15 to 18 yards from the LOS for the receiver to clear the defender.

Approach: The receiver should explode off of the line in the same manner as on the "Quick Out" move. With his inside foot back, he should drive upfield for three steps, breaking outside on the third step. He should then make a three-step drive toward the sideline as in the "Quick Out" to sell that move to the defender. As he cuts he should try to gain a yard or so upfield on the outside fake (he shouldn't break parallel to the LOS). If he looks back at the passer on this outside fake, the defender has to commit to break up the pass or keep the gain minimal. The receiver then breaks upfield on his third step to the outside—one, two, three steps up and one, two, three steps out, breaking upfield on the sixth step of the route, the left foot. Coming out of the "out" move, the receiver has to strive for full speed as soon as possible, as shown in Figure 3-3.

Breaking Point: As the receiver turns upfield he may get bumped by the defensive back, who may realize (too late if the fake was well executed) that he's been faked. The receiver has to drive through any contact and accelerate. Many experienced defensive backs, when realizing they are out of position, will manage to initiate some contact in an attempt to spoil the timing of the route. When looking back while running for the ball, the receiver must *maintain top speed*. Unitas put this pass into the air with such good timing that I seldom had to run more than 20 yards after the breaking point before the ball arrived.

    Catch: Drills that help receivers prepare for this catch are

Inside Shoulder	End Line Toe Dance
Directly Overhead	Tightrope Toe Dance
Harassment	

    Quarterback: Since this pattern doesn't require a long throw, the ball shouldn't be in the air for more than 30 yards. The quarterback should try to drop it over the receiver's head, keeping him running straight ahead or veering toward the outside. A simple way to emphasize this to your quarterback is to tell him to keep the ball out in front of his receiver's outside shoulder. Placing the ball in this manner makes it very difficult for a defender to break up the throw even if he is in fairly good position. Leading the receiver inside makes it easier on the defender in most cases as it places him in the passing lane. A point to emphasize as well is that the pass should have a lot of arch; it cannot be a line drive type pass.

    When Unitas released the ball he had it away in less than 2.5 seconds, which didn't require a lot of pass protection. He didn't wait for the receiver to break wide open, but released the ball as soon as the receiver turned upfield. He also compensated on his throw if the defensive man bumped the receiver coming off of the break. He took something off of the throw and also laid it a little more to the outside.

    Your quarterback should be aware of whether or not the defender is watching him or keying the receiver. If he is watching the quarterback, he should fake a throw (pump) at the receiver when he makes his outside drive fake. The defender will more than likely react as much to the throwing fake as to the receiver's outside move. If the defender is watching the receiver, then the quarterback doesn't need to pump, but he may want to look off a free safety in this situation. There should be some "Quick Outs" completed before this move; in other words the defender should be set up. If he continues to lay back, however, continue to take what he is giving—the "Quick Out."

The "Quick Out and Post"

Purpose of the Route: To take advantage of a defender who is reacting hard to the outside when your receiver runs the "Quick Out." If the defender is also maintaining a good cushion of 4 to 5 yards, he is too far off to run the "Quick Out and Up," but his reaction *and* cushion allow the receiver to fake him badly and break back *under* him to the post area *without* bumping into him. This move cannot be run unless the defenders in the inside area are occupied, or unless the defense is such that the inside area is unoccupied.

Alignment: Normally the receiver will line up just as he does for the "Quick Out," since this is a counter-move and everything should look the same.

Approach: Your receiver should run everything just like the "Quick Out and Up," only for this, the receiver breaks back to the inside on a Post route on the 6th step.

Breaking Point: Coach your receivers to get back inside as fast as they can. Ideally, when he plants his foot to break, the defensive man should overrun him as he is blasting to the outside. On his approach, the receiver should have gone more straight upfield on the first three steps off of the line, inviting the defender to jump on the "Quick Out." As he breaks back inside, he takes a 45-degree angle on the Post move.

This move can be used for both a "Quick Post" type throw (with the ball drilled between the linebackers) and a

"Deep Post" throw (with the ball arched deep). Since the outside fake causes the receiver to widen to the outside, it gives him more room inside in which to operate. When the catch is made, the receiver is usually at just about the same width as when he lined up. See Figure 3-4.

Catch: Drills that help receivers prepare for this catch are:

Behind	Low Ball
Concentration	Scoop
High Look-In	Deep Inside Shoulder
High Behind	

We used this move several times inside the 5-yard line and curled in behind a tight defender rather than going *under.* The both times that a touchdown resulted, it was right on the edge of the end line and the "Toe Dance" and "High Look-In" drills paid off.

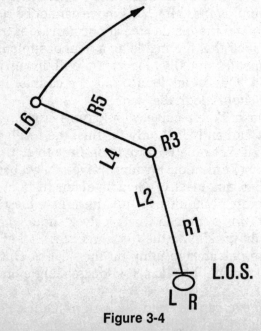

Figure 3-4

The Quick Out and Post

Quarterback: Unitas took a seven-step or nine-step drop on the "Deep Post" throw. Backs coming out of the backfield can be used to open up the post area by occupying linebackers. The release is around 2.8 seconds. The ball is away by the third step of the receiver after the breaking point. The quarterback should put some arch on the throw so that a lineman can't tip the ball, which happened to us twice. It's best to be able to use this move for a "Deep Post" route. This avoids any danger of a defensive lineman batting the ball, or of linebackers being a factor in ruining the completion.

This route has interception danger if the quarterback doesn't know what he is doing. Namely, the inside area must be cleared out. Many times in games this move would have worked but we didn't use it. The type of defense we were playing against caused too much risk.

This particular move completely fooled more defensive backs than any other I can remember. Several times they just fell down flat. The key is using it at the right time on the right guy. It takes some work to get this move down. Coming off the turn back to the inside is the tough part.

The receiver's speed has to be controlled enough on this move so that he can be deliberate on the three steps up and the three steps out, yet still be able to stop and get back inside with a minimum of delay and loss of balance.

The "Quick Post and Up"

Purpose of the Route: To get open deep. The move should be made against a corner back who is influenced by an inside fake in the 5- to 10-yard area from the LOS. The move should either completely turn him to the inside or freeze him so the receiver can get by him to the outside on the Up route. A defensive back who is playing head up is particularly vulnerable, especially if he is inside-conscious. If the defensive halfback is not reacting to an inside move, go ahead and run Curls, Turn-Ins, Hooks, Quick Posts, etc. Caution your receivers against using an inside fake on a defender who does not react, otherwise he will cram it down the receiver's throat. Otherwise, burn the defender with this move if he is going to be around the receiver's neck when he runs inside moves. The route is very simple and easily learned and doesn't require but 2.5 to 2.7 seconds of protection—maybe less if the receiver only has to go 4 or 5 yards upfield before making his inside move.

Alignment: On the short side. This is a good move because the receiver doesn't need much room to run it. If to the short side, a good split would be 8 yards from the sideline. The receiver could get 5 to 6 yards and still be okay. If the ball is in the middle, a position halfway between the hash and the sideline is good. If he is split out to the wide side, the main factor to consider is the strength of the passer's arm. Another factor to remember is that the "Quick Post and Up" is a counter-move to the inside moves, so the receiver doesn't want to tip off the defender by lining up one way for the inside moves, and lining up another way for the Up move.

Approach: If the receiver lines up with his inside foot back, he should come straight off the line anywhere from four to six steps. He should then fake inside for either one, two, or three steps. I've seen the move run all three ways and still be successful. I liked to run the route with steps of five up and two in—a seven-step move. If the defensive back was tighter, I would go three up and two in (we called this a "Look-In and Up"). I learned to "roll" inside off of my right foot (fifth step), which gave me a two-step, or left-right fake inside. I broke upfield off of the seventh step or right foot. Help your receivers work out their steps to suit their styles. I had a long stride and I found out that taking a three-step move inside on the fake was too far. It made it too hard to stop my inside momentum and get back on the Up. A one-step fake inside (six up and one in) wasn't deliberate enough to get the defender turned. The two steps in allowed me to get off of the break with speed but still be deliberate inside. (Follow outline of steps in Figure 3-5.)

A "look" fake inside when the receiver fakes inside is recommended. The receiver should whip his head inside to look for the ball. If the defender is reading the receiver's

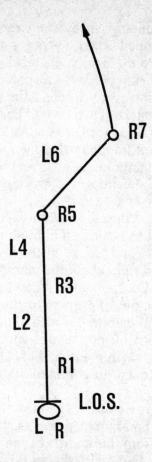

Figure 3-5

The Quick Post and Up

head, this is very important. He will usually react when he sees the receiver's head and go for the ball. This is a speed move. That's one thing I liked about it as a player. A receiver can get right on the defender, make his move and take off, hardly losing a bit of speed enroute.

The depth at which the receiver makes his move should depend on the depth of the defender. Note: He should make this move far enough away from the defender so that he doesn't get bumped when he comes off of his break.

Breaking Point: Ideally, the receiver wants the defender to be slightly inside of him as he comes off of the break. An inexperienced receiver will make the mistake of getting too far inside on his fake. Then he will be forced to make a wide detour to get around the man. Again, this move should not be attempted unless the defensive man will react inside. The first time it is attempted, the receiver might aim at the outside shoulder of the defender as a breaking point for the inside fake.

I used to be conscious of the fact that the "moment of truth" occurred as I came off of my break. Having made the inside fake, with the "look" at the quarterback, I knew I'd better have been right about the man reacting. If he didn't, I was in trouble. Consequently, when I drove off that seventh step I was conscious of dipping or pulling away toward the outside—a slight detour. On several occasions the defender got a small piece of me but not enough to keep me from getting by him. It is imperative that at this point the receiver *turn on the speed*, because from this point on he is reacting to the ball.

In Baltimore we did *not* head straight upfield after coming off of the break on Up routes. We faded toward the outside, away from the middle of the field—away from the free safety help. Our quarterbacks threw the ball, pulling us slightly toward the outside. For example, if I was running a "Quick Post and Up" on the short side of the field, I would probably line up 8 yards from the sideline boundary.

After the approach and inside fake, I would come off the break about 10 yards from the sideline. When the ball was actually caught 35 to 40 yards downfield, I would probably be only 3 to 4 yards from the sideline. The receiver should sprint for several strides before actually looking back for the ball to attain as much separation as possible from the defender. He will cover about 25 yards from the time he comes off of the break until the ball arrives. (See Figure 3-5.)

The Catch: Drills that help receivers, along with the rest of the deep drills are

Inside Shoulder

Wrong Shoulder

Directly Overhead

If the receiver is running this move from the 30-yard line in, he will need the "End Line Toe Dance." If he is on the short side of the field, the "Tightrope Toe Dance" situation will likely occur. If the ball is underthrown, the receiver and the defender will engage in a little harassment.

After the Catch: The receiver should practice on every deep route exploding after the catch. In a game, this should be automatic.

Quarterback: On this route John Unitas would set up quickly at 9 yards, move forward and throw. Emphasize to the players that he released the ball when the defender and the receiver were even with each other—about 13 yards from the LOS. Also note that this is a high-arch type pass as described above.

The "Look-In and Up Sideline"

Purpose of the Route: This is a 15- to 18- yard sideline route that is supposed to look like the receiver is going deep on a "Look-In and Up." It is supposed to get the defender to turn to the inside and look for the receiver to try to beat him deep.

Alignment: Since the approach will bring the receiver a yard or two in from his initial alignment, he can split slightly wider. If he is on the short side of the field, he can line up 6 or 7 yards from the sideline. When he comes off of the break at 15 to 18 yards deep, he should be about 8 yards from the boundary. This will give him enough room to catch the ball before he goes out of bounds. If the ball is in the middle of the field, he should split about halfway between the hash mark and the sideline. When he comes off of his break, he should have about 11 yards to his outside. This will help your quarterback by giving him enough room to lead the receiver properly while not being out of range. If he has a hard time reaching the receiver, the split can be cut down. If the receiver is split to the wide side of the field, the receiver should line up on the hash mark and see if that is okay with the quarterback. If not, cut it down. A factor that will alter this distance is whether or not the quarterback is rolling toward the receiver on a play action or sprint out. If this is the case, then the alignment can be adjusted a little wider.

Approach: This is a speed route. The receiver should really explode off of the line. My steps on this route were three steps up, roll off of the third step, two steps on the fake to the inside, plant on the fifth or right foot, take off deep and break outside on the ninth step—three steps up, two in, four up and out. I gave a "look" fake on the inside fake. Your receivers can vary their steps to suit their strides. Basically, they are going upfield 4 or 5 yards, fake in, then burst up. A receiver with a lot of speed can go deeper, perhaps, than one with very limited speed. For example, a boy with a 4.6 or 4.7 second speed can run this route and go 18 yards, and the passer can put the ball in the air in 2.8 seconds. A boy with a 5-second flat speed may only need to go 13 to 14 yards deep to keep it a 2.8 second throw. A sprint out will often give the receiver more time, as well as the passer.

Breaking Point: The fundamentals for the receiver to remember are speed off of the break and to get his head around quickly to pick up the ball. Whether the receiver should cut squarely to the sideline or round it out is a good point to consider. There seems to be two ways to approach this, and I've seen both used successfully. By not being concerned about a square cut, the receiver will maintain full stride and the speed threat and just "roll" to the outside. The defender gets no clue from a "gathering" motion. If you desire a square cut, then most receivers are going to have to "gather" themselves for two or three short strides. This is necessary in order to cut their speed so they can make a square cut. I don't believe there are many receivers who can be blasting along at full speed at 15 to 18 yards and without any preliminary indication just cut to the outside at 90 degrees as illustrated in Figure 3-6. One advantage of using the "gather" technique is that the quarterback gets a clue or key that tells him the break is coming. I believe he can get the ball off with a little better timing, thereby not requiring as much room to the outside.

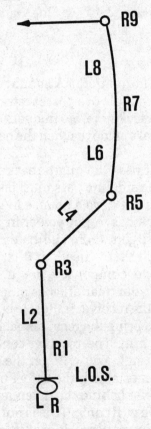

Figure 3-6

The Look-In and Up Sideline

The distance covered from the break to the catch, if the ball is thrown on good timing (which means just as the receiver is breaking to the outside), will be 8 to 10 yards. The receiver must run full speed until he is sure the ball is not too far out in front of him.

The Catch: Drills that will help your receivers prepare for the route are:

High Back to the Passer	High and Behind
Low Ball	Scoop
Back to the Passer	One Hand
Concentration	Toe Dance
Holler Ball	

Quarterback: The quarterback should drop back 9 yards. Unitas was a great example of a passer releasing the ball with perfect timing. His receivers were frequently one stride away from making the final out move when the ball actually left his hand.

On this type of pass the quarterback can't afford to be late in throwing. The sideline pass must be timed so that the defensive back does not have a chance to get a jump on the ball. The quarterback has to put power into this throw, and the quicker the ball gets there the better. The longer the throw, the more arch that is needed. It takes a good arm to throw outside, so to compensate for a possible lack of strength, make sure your quarterbacks practice releasing the ball very quickly. If the receiver is closely covered, the passer can throw it low and bring the receiver back or throw it high and out in front of him. The receiver can get to it but the defensive halfback can't. You will get the best results from this route if you first establish the threat of the deep route. Once you get a receiver behind the defender on the "Look-In and Up," the sideline will come. This is not difficult to learn, although deep sideline patterns do require more pass protection.

The "Slant Jab Look-In"

Purpose of the Route: The "Look-In" is a quick inside move designed to attack the area between the linebackers and in front of the defensive backs. The "Slant Jab" approach is simply to give a little variation to the move in order to set up a great sideline move versus man-to-man, called the "Slant Jab Sideline."

Alignment: If the intended receiver is the flanker, he will line up wider than the split end. If he is on the short side, he should split from 5 to 8 yards from the sideline. If the ball is in the middle, the split should be halfway between the hash and the sideline. If he is split to the wide side, split him to the hash. These are just some guidelines which are subject to change depending on the abilities of the personnel. However, the receiver should never vary his stance so that he is tipping off his intentions. He should line exactly the same way when running the "Slant Jab Look-In" (Figure 3-7a) and the "Slant Jab Sideline." (Figure 3-7b). The two go together —move and counter-move—so everything must start out the same to have the most success against the defender.

Approach: The receiver's approach on this move should be inside immediately. This gains inside position for the receiver on the defender covering him. He is moving with speed. The last step is the Jab step—it is the last thing he does before the "Look-In" route. My steps were three inside and one directly at the defender. The jab step freezes or rocks back a defensive back if he is reacting to the receiver and is fairly close. The receiver must make a move at him but continue on inside rapidly, looking for the ball. Again, the move isn't so much to help him get open on the "Look-In" as it is to get the defender used to seeing him do it going inside. Later, when he sees the receiver use the exact approach he will think inside which will help set up the sideline pattern.

The receiver's angle as he leaves the line is not too severe. Note this in Figures 3-7a and 3-7b. I used to look inside on my initial move off of the line and then look right at the defender on my jab step at him.

Breaking Point: Ideally, the defensive halfback should be a couple of steps to the receiver's outside at this point. Teach your receivers to whip the head around quickly for the

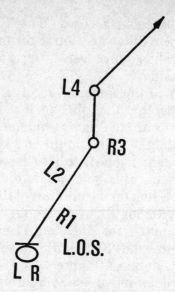

Figure 3-7a

The Slant Jab Look-In

ball. The break occurs at about 5 yards deep and the catch is made at 10 yards as shown in Figures 3-7a and 3-7b.

The Catch: Usually the ball will arrive just a moment before the pursuit. Concentration on the ball is a must. Drills that will help your receivers prepare for this route are

High Look-In	High Behind
Low Ball	Scoop
Behind	One Hand
Holler Ball	Concentration

The "End Line Toe Dance" drill is good if the pattern is run near the Goal Line. When working on this pattern, it is a good time to emphasize to your receivers not to run with the ball before it is caught, and to put both hands on it whenever they are in a crowd.

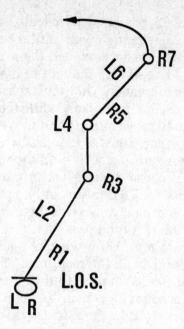

Figure 3-7b

The Slant Jab Sideline

After the Catch: Sometimes on this route a receiver will make the catch and have an opportunity to run with the ball. If he can make the first tackler miss him he can have some real fun. This is another instance like coming off of a breaking point—it is important for him to attain top speed at once.

Quarterbacks: When running this pattern you may want to run a back in a pattern to the same side. Using flare control in this manner will help your quarterback decide who to deliver the ball to. If the running back is in a flare to the wide side, the quarterback can look to that side exclusively. He will key the linebacker on that side. If the linebacker ignores the flare and drops back into the "Look-In" area, hit the back. If the linebacker moves for the flare, the "Look-In" will be open. The linebackers must be controlled to open up the inside passing lanes.

Inexperienced passers will usually wait too long to throw the ball. They tend to wait until the receiver becomes open between the linebackers, and then throw. They must learn to see the linebackers moving to the outside and the receiver starting to come in. They must release the ball *before* the receiver clears the linebacker. While the ball is in the air, the linebacker will move outside and the receiver will move inside about 5 yards. He will be open when he makes the catch. If your quarterbacks wait until the receiver is open to throw, they will cause the receiver to move about 5 yards farther to the inside. That means only one thing—the next inside linebacker or safety man will then be in good position to break up or intercept the pass.

A quarterback must know what he's going to do in order to throw inside and avoid interceptions. There are just more people to the inside. When he throws deep or outside, he doesn't have to account for as many people. Even though this is a simple move to run, the passer will have to practice against a live defense to really learn how to time the throw and *see* it develop.

Three Ways to Run a Turn-In

1. Jab Out and Up Turn-In
2. Bend Out Turn-In
3. Slant Burst Turn-In

These three routes are separate and distinct methods of attacking the same general area of the secondary. You may want to incorporate one, two, or all three in your passing offense. All three include similar approaches to other routes included in this chapter. Each route employs more than one fake to set the defender up for the final cut. While these routes may appear complicated, they can be learned quickly through exact repetition. Once the receiver has the feel for balance and speed throughout the moves he will break wide open because of the fakes leading up to the final cut.

1. Jab Out and Up Turn-In

Purpose of the Route: From the time the receiver leaves the line of scrimmage until he gets to his breaking point, he will have run two outside fakes. He will have widened about 3 yards to get the defender moving to the outside or to turn him to the outside so the receiver can then break back under him. The receiver is trying to lure the defender out of position. This is an outside approach to run an inside move. Receivers can use the exact same move to run an out. A receiver should not use this approach for a "Turn-In" until he has tested it on the defender beforehand. He can use this move when running deep on a screen pass or when working downfield during the game. If the defender opens up or turns and moves to the outside with the receiver, then you know the "Jab Out and Up" approach will help the receiver on a "Turn-In." This same approach can be used for a post or in route. Since most turn-in routes are not exact "throw on the break" routes, the move will not affect the quarterback's timing. Emphasize to your receivers not to use this move until they are sure the defender will react in such a way that the move will be successful. If they don't, it will put them in a bad position.

Alignment: One advantage of the move for the receiver is that it widens him, gives him more room inside. This helps on inside routes. Since the quarterback will be throwing in the lane between the linebackers, it helps widen the lane. Split rules vary, but here are some that receivers may use: If split out on the short side of the field, split about 8 yards from the sideline. If the ball is in the middle, split about halfway between the hash mark and the sideline. If split out to the wide side of the field, line up on the hash mark.

Approach: This move is not the simplest to run. It takes some repetition to get it down. I tried to get 10 to 12 yards depth on the route and my steps are illustrated in Figure 3-8.

Your receivers may be short striders and may take more steps to get the same depth. For example, a receiver may

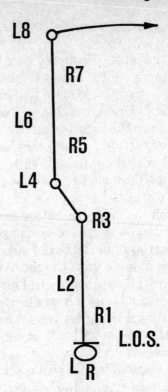

Figure 3-8

The Jab Out and Up Turn-In

make his first fake off of his fifth step. I made it off of my third.
I just jabbed out one step and then drove upfield again. The
defender gets the impression that the receiver is going deep.
Sometimes the receiver will need a slight fake to the outside
on the break, but if the defender is already fooled he
shouldn't bother. When first working on the break back to the
inside, the receiver should control his speed on the last step
or two before the break. As will usually be the case, once he
gets familiar with the move, he will be able to do it faster and
faster.

2. Bend Out Turn-In

Purpose of the Route: Same thoughts as on the "Jab Out and Up Turn-In," and the alignment is the same as well.

Approach: The receiver drives straight upfield about 5 yards. With my steps this took three strides and I "Bent Out" off of that third step. I made a three-step drive on that outside angle and planted on my sixth step—my left or outside foot as illustrated in Figure 3-9. I had a good bit of speed by this time and it took me a couple of steps more to get where I could plant and break back inside. This is not a difficult move to run, but it will take a little practice to make the turn and keep balance. This move can be utilized for an "out" route or a "post" route.

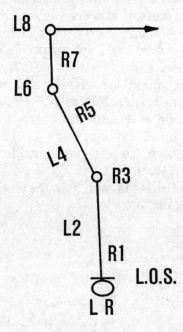

Figure 3-9
The Bend Out Turn-In

3. Slant Burst Turn-In

Purpose of the Route: On this route the receiver is working the defender inside by 2 or 3 yards, then making a "Jab"
step fake at him to freeze him or rock him back. Ideally, the
receiver should get a 2- or 3-yard advantage on him to the
inside. This approach can be used to run a "post" route, too.
The receiver could make the same approach and "jab" in to
run a good sideline route.

Alignment: Since this move brings the receiver inside
by 2 or 3 yards, I wouldn't run this on the short side of the
field unless you split him really wide, like 3 or 4 yards from
the boundary. If the ball is in the middle of the field, line him
up wider than normal for a "Turn-In." The same thing ap-
plies if the receiver is set out to the wide side of the field.

Approach: Again, the receiver is working to get about 12
yards depth. If he wants to go deeper he just needs to drive
further upfield before the final break. He should come off
with speed and drive inside with three to five steps at a slight
angle, then burst upfield for at least four strides, maybe more
if he is a short strider. (See Figure 3-10.) If he feels a good jab
fake to the outside will help him at the breaking point, he
needs to gather for a couple of steps just before making that
jab. He should then jab and break inside, which is not a
difficult move to learn.

The Catch: Drills that will help the receivers prepare for
this catch in a game are

High Look-In	High Hook
High Behind	Low Ball
Scoop	Behind
One Hand	Concentration
Holler Ball	Toe Dance (near the end zone)

Quarterback: In the last quarterback section, throwing
the inside pass was emphasized. The quarterback should
release the ball before the receiver actually gets open in the
lane between the linebackers. The other receivers must oc-

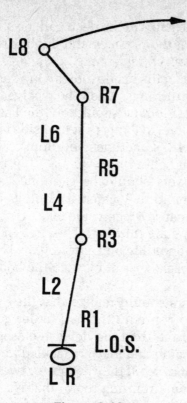

Figure 3-10
The Slant Burst Turn-In

cupy defenders to get one man open. Most "Turn-In" routes are thrown in 2.5 to 2.8 seconds. The deeper the receiver runs the patterns, the more time needed. The quarterback should never force the ball. Instead, he must look to his alternate receiver if the number one is covered.

Running with the Ball

The key word is speed—speed and explosion after the catch is made. The receiver must take off for that goal line. In the process of catching the ball the receiver will usually lose some speed. Very few passes will allow him to catch the ball without breaking stride. Consequently, the defender is going to be closing the gap. On the deep ball, he should explode as soon as he makes the catch. On the sideline routes, he should explode and turn upfield immediately after the catch. The same holds true for the inside routes. On a short hitch pass, or hooks, curls, or turnings, when the receiver catches the ball in a stopped position, he should put the ball away securely and get out of there. Making a slight inside fake and pivoting to the outside will sometimes help him elude the defender coming up from behind him.

Your receivers should be cautioned against running with the ball before they catch it. Seeing some open room will sometimes cause a receiver to take his eyes off of the ball in eagerness to start running. This ties in very well with fundamentals of holding and carrying the ball—keep a tight grip front and back; keep it close to the body, especially in traffic.

All receivers should realize that they will get limited opportunities to run with the ball under game conditions. The majority of the time the defense closes in on them so quickly after a catch that they are tackled immediately, with no chance to get away. If they get one or two opportunities a game to have some running room, that is above average.

Because of this I think it is really important that a receiver get in the habit (in practice) of not only exploding after the catch, but also running with the ball after the catch a few times a day. I mean cutting and maneuvering, stopping and starting, and then sprinting with the ball under his arm. It doesn't make any difference if there are defenders in the area or not. He should just act like they are there and develop the habits of ball carrying so that in a game he will react automatically and instinctively do the proper things. As a rule, you play like you practice.

Downfield Blocking

There are many reasons why receivers need to be effective blockers. They all add up to *winning*—that's the main reason. Following are a few basic rules:

1. When the receiver leaves the huddle he must believe that this play will be the one where the back will break into the secondary, and his block can spring him for extra yardage and perhaps a touchdown. He must assume this on every play to make the big play that will win for you.

2. He must come off of the line fast. The defender should not be able to tell any difference in his speed on running plays or passes.

3. As your receiver goes for his man, the approach angle will depend on the probable path of the ball carrier. Understanding the play, experience, and the study of game films should teach him this. Sometimes the receiver will go straight ahead and sometimes he will go at an angle as he anticipates the ball carrier's moves.

4. He should get his eyes on the defender. Caution receivers, especially, against the major error of sneaking a peek and looking back to see where the ball carrier is. This can cause the receiver to lose position on the defender. Instead, he should watch the eyes and face of his man. They will tell him when the ball carrier is behind him.

5. *The Attack and Block:* Usually receivers are blocking against the quickest and most agile people on the defense, so they cannot be expected to knock them down every time. The timing of the attack is one of the keys. Ideally, if the receiver will attack at the same time the ball carrier is there, his block will have maximum effect. One of the things he wants to avoid is attacking too early, going to the ground, and allowing the defense halfback to be free to make the tackle. If his man is giving ground, he should stay up and after him. If he freezes or tries to come through the receiver or across his path, he should cut him down. He should get close (close enough to step on the defender's toes) before uncoiling and leaving his feet. He follows up his block by rolling after him.

Additional tips for the receivers: A wide base with short steps in the attack area may help keep the receiver from getting faked out of position. He should keep his head up and hold up if the defender gets his back to him to avoid the clip.

As he is stalking his man, both of them may break down for a moment and the receiver shouldn't wait too long before attacking. Again, he should try to time it so that he gets into the defender just before the ball carrier arrives, and sustain his block as long as he can. His final effort, his final nudge, may get just enough of the defender to allow the ball carrier to slip free for a long gain or a touchdown. When the receiver is on the side away from the point of attack, it is still important for him to get his man. Should the ball carrier get away, the backside defender will be the last man blocked in order for the back to go all the way.

Pass receivers should take great pride in being complete football players. This begins with taking pride in blocking. Their teammates like to see them getting after the folks downfield. The defense does not like to see this. A receiver must believe his block will be the one to spring the back for the touchdown.

Coaching the Tight End as Receiver

4

CHARACTERISTICS OF THE POSITION

The tight end position requires a very special type of athlete. Not only must he be capable of going down inside and blocking much bigger defensive linemen, but he must be a respectable pass-receiving threat. The tight end is usually the slowest receiver on the field as well as being the biggest. Since he cannot rely as much on speed to help him get open, he must execute his routes extremely well. The advantage he has is size—he will usually be covered downfield by a smaller defensive back. He can frequently "muscle" the ball away from a defender.

From his position, he can rarely release from the line with ease because of linebackers or defensive ends that are assigned to hold him up on every play. When he does release into the secondary, he, too, is faced with a quick defender covering him. He is not able to see the entire defense as the quarterback does. He is frequently a major key for the defensive secondary and is seldom open for any great length of time. However, an advantage is his proximity to the quarterback. He doesn't have to be as open since the ball usually doesn't have as far to go to reach him. A tight end is in ideal position to catch a lot of passes.

When not in a route, the tight end is expected to be a good blocker, not only for the running game, but frequently for passes where only one or two receivers are in a pattern. He must be rugged because he receives solid contact on every play.

While often selected for his size and blocking ability, the tight end should be a disciplined receiver capable of getting open for the short pass over the middle, in the flat, deep in the middle of the field, and deep to the outside of the field. Sometimes he will be aligned as the inside receiver, as in a flanker set; and sometimes as the only receiver on his side, as in a slot set. Frequently, the difference in sets will be met with a different defensive alignment opposite the tight end. He must learn to recognize the alignments he faces and who will be covering him, or the area he will be going into.

Your tight end bears a big responsibility to the offense and should be constantly encouraged to be proficient at all phases of his position.

ALIGNMENT—CAPITALIZE ON WHAT
THE DEFENSE GIVES

The tight end can have a great deal of influence on the defensive alignment, no matter what play is to be run. He should be aware of this and be encouraged to experiment with his line split when not directly involved in the blocking at the point of attack. He may discover that he can create or emphasize a weakness in the defense by stretching the off-tackle gap or by gaining outside leverage on the line. Once a weakness is discovered or established, it can be exploited by the pass and the run, both to the tight end side and away, so that the defense cannot read his split variations.

He doesn't have to be as concerned with the football's lateral position on the field as a wide receiver does. Normally, he will have sufficient room to execute all of his patterns regardless of being lined up on the short side of the field. As all receivers should, he should be aware of how he is being defensed—zone or man-to-man or combination; as well as how the individual defenders are playing him—inside shade, outside shade, loosely or tightly. He, along with the quarterback, should be able to recognize what the defense is giving him.

STANCE—THE BALANCED BEGINNING OF EVERY PLAY

Many offenses feature a tight end who flip-flops depending on the play. For a normal right-handed tight end, the most common stance for overall effectiveness—run and pass—is a stance with right foot staggered no more than right toe, to left heel with the right hand down. The weight should be fairly evenly distributed on all three points. (*Coaching Point:* a smart defender may look at your end's fingers on the ground to determine if he varies the amount of weight he has forward. Caution your player to be careful and consistent.)

Tight ends really have to discipline themselves in the development of their stances. Their position requires them to fire off the line straight ahead to block, step inside to block down, step or pull outside to block outside, and to get off of the line for a pass play. If not careful, a tight end can develop a stance for each responsibility and the defense will read him like a book. One good method to help him develop the balanced uniform stance is to have him take his stance before he knows his assignment. Drilling in this manner early in the season will quickly help him acquire a good stance.

RELEASING—BREAKING OFF OF THE LINE INTO THE ROUTE

The tight end will nearly always have a man assigned to delay him in getting off of the line. He may have to widen his split some in order to get some room to operate. As explained above, this can be done without tipping the defense. If it is an obvious passing situation—the defense knows that you have to pass—the tight end could be taught to go ahead and take a split that aids his release. Quickness is vital. He must get off on the snap count to have a chance to take the initiative away from the defender who is trying to hold him up. He can utilize the same release fakes the wide receivers use to escape a tight defender.

If the defense assigns a man to delay your wide receivers from getting off of the line, your receivers will need some quick fakes to escape. Quickness is vital, so the receiver must explode on the snap count. The release fakes shown in Figure 3-1 are for a receiver on the left side. By practice and repetition a receiver can develop these to the degree that he can execute them quickly and still maintain good balance. Stress to your receivers that if a defender walks right up onto their nose that they have to even up their stance—get both feet even or nearly so—to allow movement quickly either in or out.

The tight end should become very conscious of the use of his arms as another technique in releasing from the line of scrimmage. For example, if the tight end is aligned on the left side and he is going to release to his outside left, he can bring his right arm upward with his first step. Whether or not this step is a lead step or a crossover, he needs to use his right arm to keep the defender from putting his hands on the tight end and controlling his first few steps off of the line. It will be harder for the defender to make solid contact with the tight end if he will stay low for the first two or three steps off of the line.

The "Drag Out"

Purpose of the Route: To attack the short flat area. The defense is not adequately covering with linebackers and the outside defenders can be taken out of the area by a wide receiver. This is an excellent tight end pattern, whether or not the tight end is to the short side or the wide side of the field. If a receiver is flanked outside the tight end, this route becomes an underneath route for the flanker, who runs and puts additional pressure quickly on the flat. When the tight end is the lone receiver on his side, this pattern should be as effective as that to the wide side.

This is an excellent route for the tight end when combined with play action to the strongside off-tackle hole, since the linebacker or defensive back who is expected to help support the off-tackle run is frequently responsible for the flat to the two-receiver side. He can't be two places at once.

Alignment: To execute the "Drag" route, the tight end can line up just like he has been doing on his blocking assignments—his normal alignment.

Release: Outside.

Approach: Your tight end should come off the line fast, hard, and low. As a general rule, the tight end should try to sell the pass when he is going off of the line to block; and he should try to sell the run when he releases for a pass. The tight end should drive right at the safety's outside shoulder or directly at him. If he is 6 or more yards off of the line it probably won't make any difference. This is an excellent three-step move for the tight end with his inside foot back on the left side; and a four-step move with his outside foot back on the right side. On either side he drives off of his left foot—the first step with his right foot. This will allow him to break sharply to the outside off of his inside foot. If he stays low on his release, he will not have to gather to make the break and tip off the defender.

The "Drag Out" is a good pattern when the tight end has someone lined up on his outside shoulder who is going to try to hold him up on the line or force him to release inside. The route will time out the same if his first step is inside to avoid the chuck at the line. He continues the pattern for two or three steps upfield before breaking sharply for the sideline.

Breaking Point: After planting the inside foot to cut, the tight end should explode to the outside with as much speed as possible, as illustrated in Figure 4-1a. The defender must be inside-conscious of the tight end at all times, regardless of his release, because he is a constant inside threat. The tight end should break open on his cut and the passer will most likely put the ball out in front of him. The receiver must anticipate this and get his head around quickly to pick up the flight of the ball. This will be a relatively close pass for the quarterback but he will have to deliver the ball sharply. If the quarterback will not hesitate or try to force the ball if his receiver is covered, this is not a risky pattern for the tight end on the two-receiver side of the formation or on the side opposite of a slot set.

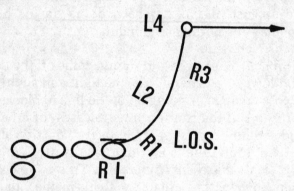

Tight Ends have an even stance usually, rather than a staggered stance. There might be a slight stagger—right foot slightly back if the right hand is down.

Figure 4-1a

The Drag Out

In addition, the "Drag Route" by the tight end can be used primarily to help the flanker's route. In other words, the object of the pass is to get the ball to the flanker on an individual move like a curl. The tight end is run into the area to draw coverage away from the flanker. The quarterback will stay with the flanker and go to the tight end only if the defense ignores him. In this case the tight end will "throttle" his speed as he nears the boundary and simply wait for a possible throw from the quarterback. See the companion routes with the "Drag Out," Figures 4-1b through 4-1e.

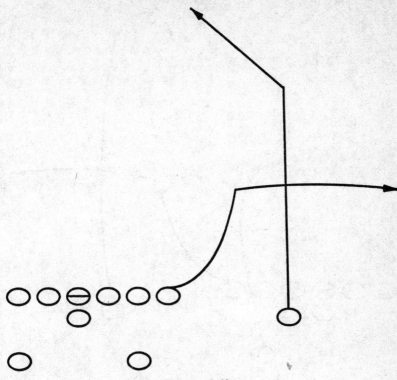

Figure 4-1b

**Companion Route with Drag
Out**

The Catch: The tight end has to get his head around quickly and watch the ball into his hands; then tuck it away quickly and tightly. Catching drills that will help your receivers prepare for this route are

High Back to the Passer	Holler Ball
High and Behind	Concentration
Behind	Low Ball
One Hand	Scoop
Toe Dance	Back to the Passer

After the Catch: Have your receivers practice turning upfield for extra yardage. Have them work on some moves to

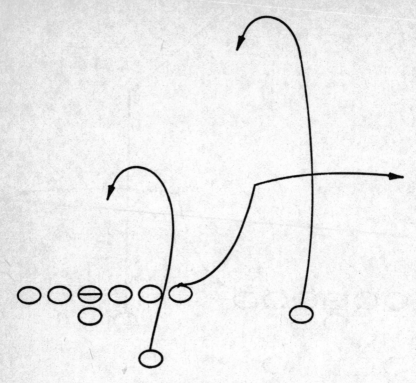

Figure 4-1c

**Companion Route with Drag
Out**

elude tacklers: fake inside, go outside; or fake upfield and cut
back inside. They need to practice protecting the ball and
holding the ball tightly, especially when in a crowd.

The "Drag Out and Go"

Purpose of the Route: To be used when you can predict
man coverages and to take advantage of a defender who is
trying to break up or intercept the "Drag Out." This is best for
the tight end when he is the second receiver in on his side. If
he aligns as the only receiver on one side, the defensive
corner or halfback will usually align 4 to 5 yards outside of

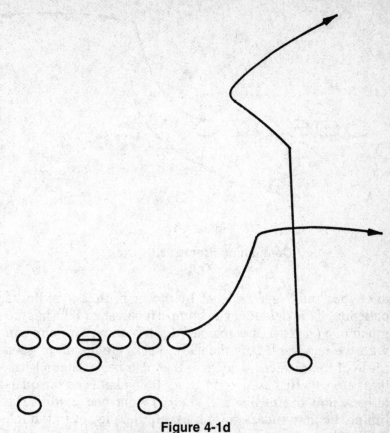

Figure 4-1d

**Companion Route with Drag
Out**

his position and will have a good cushion. When the tight
end has a flanker to his side, the flanker can draw the corner
in and the safety or linebacker then responsible for the flat or
the tight end will not have such an advantageous position at
the start of the play. This move is most effective and has its
best chance of working when the defender is tight in man-
to-man coverage and he doesn't have much cushion.

When the tight end breaks to the outside, the defensive
man is within 2 to 3 yards of the receiver and reacting hard to
the "out" move. The key is that the tight end can turn upfield

Figure 4-1e

**Companion Route with Drag
Out**

after the "out" fake and get by the man, thus avoiding a collision. If the defender can bump a receiver, or if he has too much of a cushion, it is too easy for him to recover and run with the receiver. Many defensive backs are taught to get a piece of the receiver whenever they can because good patterns are usually based upon good timing between the quarterback and the receiver. If the defender can disrupt the timing, he may successfully break up the play even though he may be out of position.

Alignment: For the best chance of success, you would want to align the tight end and the flanker to the wide side of the field. The tight end should be nearly even with the defender when he makes his "out" move. If the defender runs parallel to him to cover the "out" instead of taking a slight pursuit angle, he will be beat when the tight end turns upfield. The tight end must sell the "out" on his fake to get the defender moving at full speed.

Release: Outside.

Approach: Again, the player's speed off of the line is essential. If he is on the left side, the tight end should drive upfield for three steps, making everything look exactly like the "Drag Out." He drives toward the sideline just like in the "Drag Out" while trying to gain about a yard upfield on this fake. He should practice a quick look back at the passer on the outside fake as if he is expecting the ball. If the defender is keying the man he will look also. The tight end breaks on the "Go" when his third step to the outside hits—one, two, three steps off of the line, and one, two, three steps out with a look fake; then break up again on the third outside step. He should accelerate upfield right out of the break. See Figures 4-2a and 4-2b.

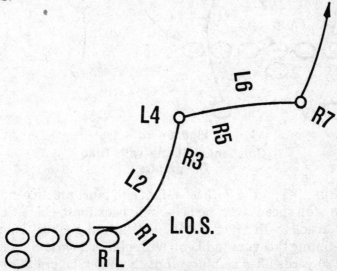

Figure 4-2a

The Drag Out and Go

Breaking Point: As the tight end turns upfield he may get a bump from the defender when he realizes that he has been beaten. Some practice time should be devoted to teaching the receivers to drive through any contact and run. This could be incorporated into the "Concentration" drill, because in many instances the ball will be just leaving the quarterback's hand. The receiver's concentration has to be focused on the ball, and not broken by any contact.

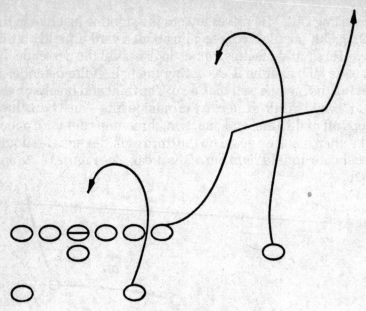

Figure 4-2b
Companion Route with Drag
Out and Go

Running for the Ball: The tight end must practice maintaining top speed when he is looking back for the ball. Good quarterbacks will often put the ball into the air with such good timing that your tight end will seldom have to run more than 20 yards after coming off of the break before the ball actually arrives. Therefore, this route can work from the 15 to 20 yard lines if the defense is in man coverage.

The Catch: Drills that will help your tight ends prepare for game situations on this pattern are:

Inside Shoulder   End Line Toe Dance

Directly Overhead   Tightrope Toe Dance

Harassment

Quarterback: This throw to the tight end does not require a long throw. The ball shouldn't have to be in the air more than 30 yards. The quarterback should try to drop it in over the receiver's head, keeping him running straight ahead or veering toward the outside. Your quarterback will be able to read the defender on the "out" fake and then react to the defender's position, deciding whether to throw to the tight end or not. When he throws the ball, placement can make it even more difficult on the defender even if he is fairly close. The ball should arch and lead the tight end slightly to the outside.

This is a timing pattern. The quarterback has to have the pass away in about 2.5 seconds. That doesn't require much protection because he doesn't wait until the tight end breaks wide open. As soon as the tight end turns upfield, he releases. If the receiver gets bumped at the breaking point, the quarterback should compensate on his throw by taking something off and laying the ball a little more to the outside.

The quarterback must know who the defender is keying—the quarterback or the receiver. If he is keying the quarterback, the quarterback can use a pump fake at the tight end on the "out" move to really sell it to the defender, who will react as much to the throwing motion as to the receiver's fake. If the defensive back is keying the receiver, then the pattern should be sufficient in itself to get the receiver open. The quarterback has to be concerned with a free safety coming into the area to help. This can be avoided by having your quarterback look off any other defender who is keying him.

Usually there should be some "Drag Outs" completed before this route is attempted. These passes will be completed in front of the defensive man. Work two or three patterns to set him up—get him concerned about stopping the "Drag Out" and he will be looking for it. If he is expecting it, then he will go for the fake to the outside and the "go" segment of the pattern will be open. However, if the defensive back insists upon staying back to protect the deep route then continue to throw what he is giving, in other words, keep the quarterback throwing short.

The "Drag Out and Post"

Purpose of the Route: For man-to-man coverages with no deep post defender. This route takes advantage of a defender who is reacting hard to the outside or is aligned to the outside to take away the "Drag Out" route. The defensive man is reacting hard to the outside as well as maintaining a cushion of 4 to 5 yards. He is too far off to run the "Drag Out and Go," but his reaction and the cushion allows the receiver to fake him badly outside and then break back under him to the post area *without* bumping into him. This pattern would be a good one to throw to the tight end when he is the lone receiver to his side because the two receivers to the other side should keep the inside defenders occupied, or, the secondary must be in an alignment that leaves the middle area relatively open.

Alignment: Normally the tight end should align just as he does for the "Drag Out," since this is a counter-move and you want the defender to see the same thing from your receiver. If the tight end occasionally widens his split for the "Drag Out," this is an excellent time to do the same thing.

Release: Outside.

Approach: Have your tight end run this pattern just as he would run the "Drag Out and Go," except that on this route the tight end will break back to the inside on the sixth step. A quick release is important to sell the defensive back the impression that the receiver is running the "Drag Out." With the inside foot back, the tight end drives upfield for three steps and breaks to the outside on the third step. The tight end can invite the defender to go for the "out" fake by running a little more straight upfield on his first three steps off of the line, which gives the defensive man a better angle on the "out" move. He drives for the sideline and gives a look for the ball. Again, the quarterback can pump fake at the receiver if the defender is keying the passer. The tight end then breaks back to the inside on a "post" route on his sixth step as seen in Figure 4-3.

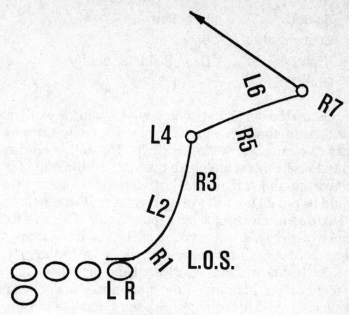

Figure 4-3

The Drag Out and Post

Breaking Point: The tight end must get back inside as quickly as he can. Ideally, when he plants to break inside, the defender should overrun him as he is blasting to the outside to break up the "out" pass. The tight end breaks inside at about a 45-degree angle. The receiver should look for the ball quickly, since the quarterback may have to throw the ball more on a line if it is to arrive before the next defender does. Ideally, you would like the pass to have some arch on it and lead the receiver upfield and a little inside if the inside is open. If the pass has to be drilled like a "Quick Post" or "Pop" route through the linebackers it must be released more quickly by the quarterback. It can also be thrown like a "Deep Post" route with deeper arch to it to lead the receiver out of secondary help.

The Catch: Drills that will help your tight end prepare for this catch in a game are:

Behind   Low Ball
Concentration   Scoop
High Look-In   Deep Inside Shoulder
High Behind

Quarterback: Unitas took a seven-step (9 yard) drop-back. The linebackers were influenced out of the area by the backs releasing out of the backfield. The ball is released at about 2.8 seconds which is the second or third step for the receiver coming off of the breaking point. Enough arch should be put on the ball to avoid having a lineman tip it. It's best to use this move for a deep "post" route. This avoids any danger of a defensive lineman batting the ball or having a linebacker recover and become a risk factor in the play.

The inside area must be cleared and there is a danger of interception on this route if the quarterback is not aware of the hazards. Also, the quarterback should not be indecisive. Indecision causes a slow release, which can allow the secondary to recover. The quarterback must be coached and have practiced what to do if the pattern is not there, or if the ball must be thrown to a certain spot to avoid interception.

It takes a lot of time to get this move down right. Coming off of the turn to get back inside quickly is the tough part. The speed is controlled enough on this move so that your tight end can be deliberate on the three steps up and the three steps out part, yet still be able to stop and get back inside with a minimum of delay and loss of balance.

The "Flag"

Purpose of the Route: To get open in the deep outside area. While the move is effective against a man-to-man defender who is influenced by an inside fake, it can also work well against a normal three deep zone. Set the tight end and the flanker on the wide side. The flanker runs a 12-yard "out" route. Against an invert zone (cornerback does not roll up, but has deep outside one-third responsibility), the quarterback keys the corner. If the corner takes the flanker, the quarterback throws to the tight end on the "Flag;" if the corner lays back, the quarterback throws to the flanker. Against a man-to-man scheme, the move should either turn the defender completely to the inside, or freeze him so that the tight end can get by him to the outside. Once the tight end clears the defender, he should look for the ball over his outside shoulder. A defensive back who lines up in a head-up position is particularly vulnerable, especially if he is inside-conscious. It is an effective route that also increases the outside effectiveness of your tight end, making his inside routes more productive as well.

Alignment: It is very important to release without getting delayed, since this is a deep route and requires more time than the other routes. This is where the tight end's knowledge of his opponent is crucial. If adjusting his split can aid in getting a fast escape, this is the time for him to do so.

Release: Coach your tight ends to release off of the line on the inside or outside—just take the fastest release they can get.

Approach: After his release, he should drive straight off of the line for four to six strides, depending on the stride of the receiver and/or the depth of the safety covering the tight end if there is man coverage. If there is man coverage, get to him and make the inside fake that is needed. It could be a quick one-step jab fake, or a two- or three-step inside fake.

Have your tight end practice a "look" fake to the inside on the inside move. If the defender is keying the receiver this is very important. He will usually react when he sees the receiver's head look for the pass. If he is keying the quarterback, a pump fake is instrumental in geting the defender turned.

This is a speed move. That's one thing I really like about this route. You can get right up on the defensive man, make your move inside, then take off and hardly lose a bit of speed during the process. The most effective weapon a receiver has against a defender is the threat of eliminating his cushion and just breaking away from him. If you can make him back up and then sell the fake, when you make the final cut it should be wide open.

The depth the tight end makes on his move will depend on the defender's depth. The tight end should make his move inside and far enough away from the defender so that the defender can't get an opportunity to bump the tight end when he comes off of his break.

Breaking Point: Ideally the defender should be aligned to the inside as the tight end comes off of his break. Another way of putting it is that the receiver wants to have "air" in front of him instead of "body." He can run through air but he wants to avoid contact with the body. An inexperienced receiver will sometimes make the mistake of getting too far inside on his fake. Then he will be forced to make a wide detour to get around the defender.

To emphasize this again, this route should not be called against man coverage unless there is good reason to believe the defensive man will react hard to the inside. To start with, you might have your receivers aim for the defender's outside shoulder as a breaking point.

I used to be conscious of the fact that the "moment of truth" occurred as I came off of my break. Having made the inside fake, with the "look" at the quarterback, I knew I'd better have been right about his reaction to the inside. If he didn't react as I'd thought, I was in trouble. Consequently, when I drove off of that break step I was conscious of dipping or pulling away toward the outside—a slight detour. On several occasions the defender got a small piece of me but not enough to keep me from getting by him. The tight end must be aware of the importance of accelerating out of the inside fake. Once he clears the defender, he is in a race for the ball. See Figures 4-4a to 4-4d for "Flag" pattern variations.

Running for the Ball: Catching the ball over the outside shoulder on a deep pass requires a "swivel" neck! You have to teach your receivers to rotate the head at an extreme angle to pick up the flight of the ball. (They can compare how

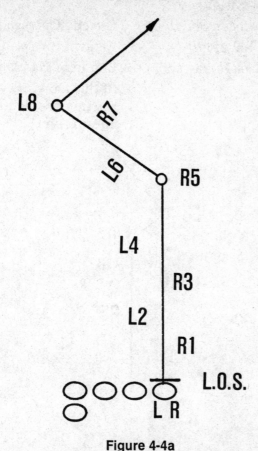

Figure 4-4a

The Flag
with Three-Step Fake Inside

simple it is to turn the head to see the ball on a deep post pattern.) The tendency is to turn the entire trunk of the body. This of course, helps them *see* the ball well enough, but it also decreases their speed a great deal. Ideally, they should keep their shoulders and arms turned straight ahead while sprinting to outrun the ball and rotate their heads and eyes only.

The Catch: Drills that will help your receivers prepare for this catch are:

Deep Outside Shoulder   Directly Overhead
Wrong Shoulder   Harassment
High Back to Passer   End Line Toe Dance
                           (If this move is ever to be
                           run from the vicinity of the
                           30 yard line.)

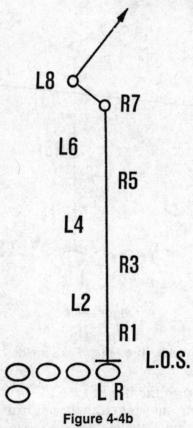

Figure 4-4b
The Flag
with One-Step Fake Inside

Quarterbacks: The quarterback must quickly set up at 9 yards deep (seven steps). He should step toward his target and throw. You want the ball released when the receiver and the defensive man are about even with each other. This

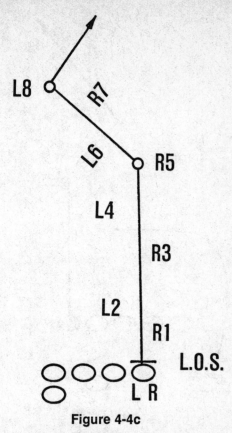

Figure 4-4c

The Flag
with Three-Step Fake Inside

should occur at about 13 yards from the line of scrimmage. The ball must have enough arch on it to carry it 25 or 30 yards from the line and it should lead the receiver slightly to the outside. If, however, the outside is covered, then the ball should be placed so as to lead the receiver to the inside a little. This will still result in a completion if the receiver has worked on the "Wrong Shoulder" drill.

The "Delay Route"

Purpose of the Route: Can be effective against either man-to-man or zone coverages. This route can be utilized

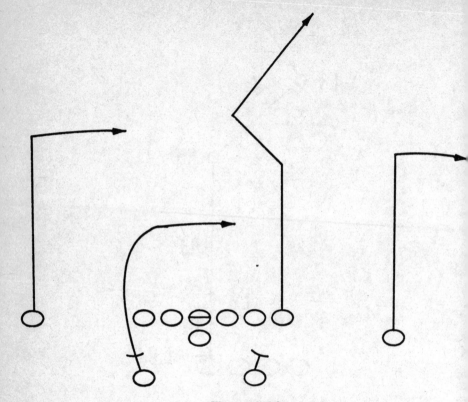

Figure 4-4d

Pattern with Flag

with a flanker to the tight end side or in a slot set with the two receivers away from the tight end. The running backs run clearing routes out of the backfield. Pass protection must allow the backs to get out unless an all-out blitz is attempted by the defense.

Alignment: Normal split, in position to block.

Release: Outside.

Approach and Breaking Point: If on the right side of the formation, release outside, drive upfield four steps and plant the left foot (fourth step). Your tight end should then break outside for two to four steps, plant his left foot and pivot or spin underneath and drive back inside. He should stay only 5 to 6 yards deep. If the defense is playing zone, he should be underneath the linebackers. If they are in man coverage, the move should help him lose the defensive back coming up to cover him. See Figures 4-5a and 4-5b.

The Catch: Drills that will help prepare your tight end for this catch in a game situation are:

High Inside   Low
Behind   High Behind
Scoop   Concentration
                   High Look-In

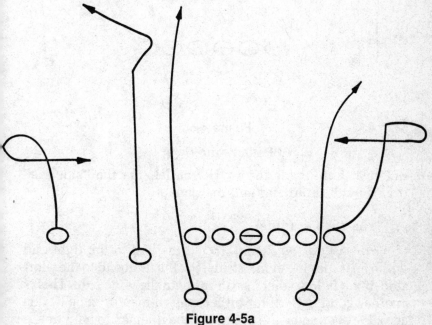

Figure 4-5a

Pattern with Delay

After the Catch: Coach your tight ends to keep both hands on the ball as they turn upfield, especially on any inside routes.

The Quarterback: He should take a seven-step or nine-yard drop. He has to allow time for the tight end to make his deliberate move. Emphasize to your quarterback that he can-

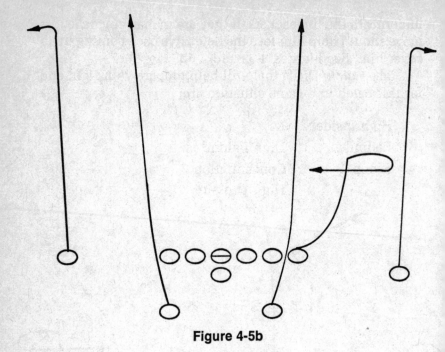

Figure 4-5b

Pattern with Delay

not rush him or his throw. His outlets are the "sideline" routes by the split end and the flanker.

The "Cross Route"

Purpose of the Route: To get the ball to the tight end while he is moving at full stride. Set the tight end to the short side of the field so that he can run into the wide side. This is another good pattern for either man-to-man or zone coverages. Play action by the backs and the linemen to help freeze the linebackers and pull them up, will open up the area for the tight end to run through.

Alignment: The tight end's alignment should be normal or he may take a slight split to aid his escape from the line.

Release: His objective is to release or escape quickly. The position of defenders on him or to his inside may vary, so the tight end or the coach should be alert for any needed adjustments. One technique is to fake a down block by stepping down with his inside foot, keeping his head and shoulders low, then knifing through the gap while staying away from the defender on him. You should teach him to use his outside arm in a backstroke motion to ward off the defender's hands. Another release would be an outside fake, inside release. If you are blessed with a tight end who is bigger and stronger than his opponent, he could just blast through the defender.

Approach and Breaking Point: The tight end should get 8 yards deep as quickly as possible, driving straight upfield. He should see the defensive back if he is covering man-to-man. If that is the case, the tight end should drive straight at him and give him an outside fake (one good jab step out with the outside foot). If he reads zone coverage, he should be alert for a linebacker on his inside. He should go behind him (over the top) if possible and then sprint across, gaining depth to 15 to 18 yards deep. See Figures 4-6a, 4-6b, and 4-6c.

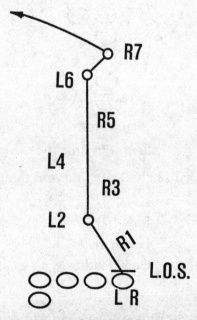

Figure 4-6a

The Cross

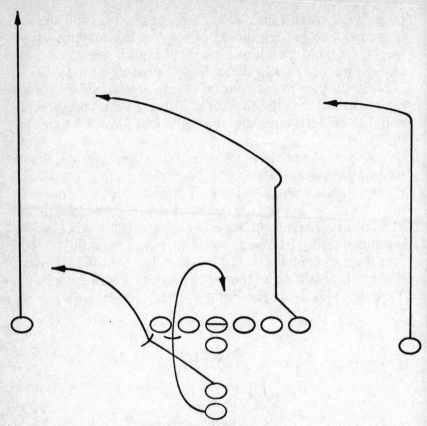

Figure 4-6b

Pattern with Cross

The Catch: Drills to help prepare your tight ends for this catch are

High Look In	Low Ball
Behind	Holler Ball
High Behind	One Hand
Concentration	

After the Catch: This can be a big gainer, with the opportunity to run with the ball, especially if the tight end comes from the short side of the field into the wide side.

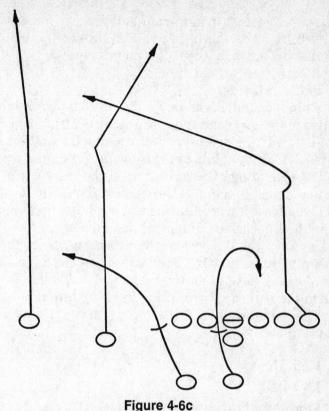

Figure 4-6c

Pattern with Cross

Quarterback: Your quarterback should make a good fake and then focus on the tight end. He should hit him on the run if he's open. An alternate receiver downfield could be the flanker coming in behind the tight end. Also, if the linebackers are deep, backs are good alternate receivers. The split end will widen the coverage by releasing outside if the corner and safety roll his way, and he continues to clear deep.

The "Curl Route"

Purpose of the Route: To get the tight end open over the middle with a route that gives him some room to maneuver against linebackers and to work to the open area. This route

works well against man-to-man and zone coverages. Your
quarterback reads the tight end and throws the ball away
from the defender (basketball-type principles).

Alignment: Normal split.

Release: Inside.

Approach and Breaking Point: You want your tight end
to drive with power and speed to a depth of 10 to 13 yards. He
should "read" the defensive back on him. If man-to-man, he
may need to drive at him or to his inside. He should try to get
the defender going backward, or try a fake outside to get him
moving in that direction. Then he should quickly stop, turn,
and come back toward the quarterback in an open lane between the linebackers. If he reads zone, he goes to an open
spot between the linebackers, turns, and waits for the ball.
Depending upon how the linebackers play the zone after he
curls, he may have to move to his right or his left, or come
back to the ball as shown in Figures 4-7a through 4-7d.

The Catch: Helpful drills to prepare your tight ends for
this catch are

High Hook
Low Ball
Concentration
Scoop

After the Catch: Since he will probably be surrounded,
the tight end must keep both hands on the ball and turn or
drive upfield to make an extra yard or yards. He must be
aware of the down and distance. He should have the first
down after the catch even if he is tackled immediately and
driven backward.

Quarterback: He should set up at seven steps or nine
yards. Since the tight end is right in front of the passer, the
throw is not difficult. He must get the knack of throwing the
ball away from the defender. With practice and "feel," your
quarterback can complete this pass even though the tight end
is closely covered. If the defender is on the tight end's right

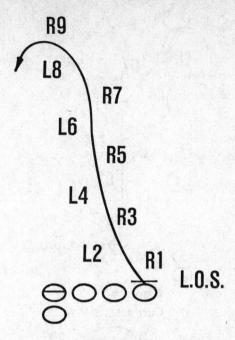

Figure 4-7a

The Curl versus Zone

side, he puts the ball on the left side of the receiver, and vice versa. (*Coaching Point:* If the tight end is in a good football stance as he maneuvers with knees bent, on his toes, then he will be able to react quickly as the quarterback places the ball.) Don Meredith used to say, "I can throw it right by a linebacker's ear at that range."

The backs are good alternate receivers. If the coverage is concentrated in the middle of the field, the wide receivers will be open.

The "Stop Route"

Purpose of the Route: To use the tight end and the split end to work on the same linebacker, one under him and one behind him. This route uses the tight end as the receiver under a linebacker to control that linebacker for the split end

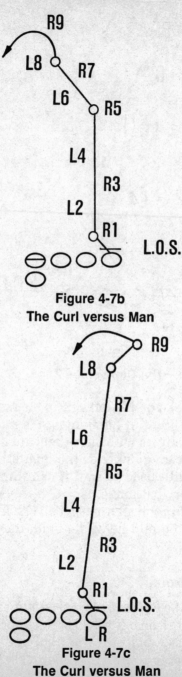

Figure 4-7b
The Curl versus Man

Figure 4-7c
The Curl versus Man

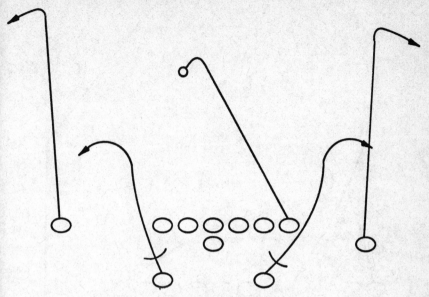

Figure 4-7d

Pattern with Curl

to "curl" behind. If the linebacker gets depth for the "curl," go to the tight end. The route is good against zone coverages.

Alignment: Normal.

Release: Inside immediately.

Approach and Breaking Point: Your tight end should aim for a point 5 yards deep, in front of his offside offensive tackle. Once he arrives at that point he stops. He waits for the ball if the quarterback has not already thrown it. (See Figure 4-8.)

The Catch: Helpful drills for the tight end:

High Hook	High Inside
Low Ball	Scoop
Behind	Concentration

After the Catch: Your tight end should get both hands on the ball as he turns upfield. He must be aware of the distance needed for the first down, especially in third down situations.

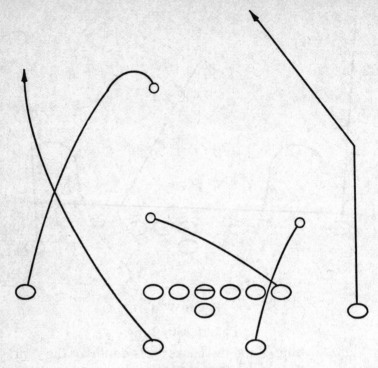

Figure 4-8

Pattern with Stop

Quarterback: He should concentrate on the linebacker covering that area, the linebacker you are picking on. If he drops deep for the "curl," he throws to the tight end on his "stop." If he is looking for the tight end, he hits the split end. If he reads blitz, he should go immediately to the "post."

The "Center Route"

Purpose of the Route: To give the tight end a route over the middle to catch the ball on the move, and enable him to run away from a man-to-man situation. This is also good versus a zone defense. This tight end route can be used in a variety of patterns for the other receivers.

Alignment: Normal position.

Release: The fastest he can get.

Approach: Your tight end has to read the strong safety to see if he is in man coverage. If so, he concentrates on an approach to beat him. See Figures 4-9a, 4-9b, and 4-9c for variations of the "center" route.

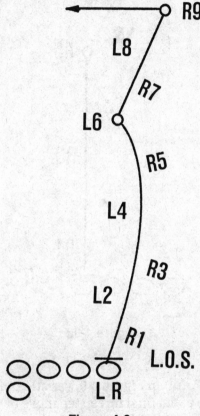

Figure 4-9a

Center

If the defense is in a zone, the tight end must be more conscious of getting his depth of at least 12 yards and widening his approach to create more throwing room over the middle between the linebackers. He should try to locate the drops of the linebackers out of the corners of his eyes as he drives upfield.

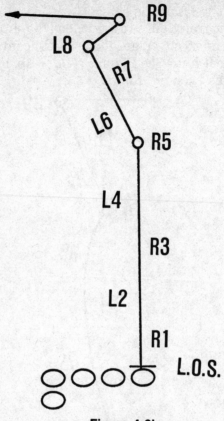

Figure 4-9b

Center

Breaking Point: In Figure 4-9, variations a, b, and c, note the importance of the final three-step move in a, and the final jab step in b and c. This is what rocks a defender back, freezes or stops him, or perhaps turns him so that the tight end creates a cushion or gap as he accelerates off of the break.

Running for the Ball: Man and zone coverages are treated differently. Versus a man coverage, your tight end will use his speed to run away from the defender; versus a zone, he may control his speed when he arrives in an open area between defenders.

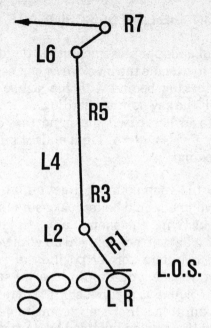

Figure 4-9c

Center

The Catch: Drills to help tight ends prepare for this catch in a game are:

High Inside	High Behind
Low Ball	Scoop
One Hand	Behind
Holler Ball	Concentration
Toe Dance	

Quarterback: Takes a seven-step or nine-yard drop. He reads zone or man-to-man coverage so that he can anticipate the type of throw needed to complete the pass to the tight end. He should try to hit him just out of his break, keeping the ball in the open lanes of the zone, or leading him away from the pursuing defensive man in man-to-man coverage.

BLOCKING ON THE LINE OF SCRIMMAGE

Most tight ends spend some time with the interior linemen learning to execute the blocking schemes of the offense. Success in blocking begins with the stance. Review with your tight ends the key points regarding stance, emphasizing consistency, regardless of whether or not they are blocking or releasing into a pass pattern. Tight ends should know these basics of blocking:

1. Know the snap count and get off on it. When a receiver is outweighed, he'd better make sure that he uses the advantage of knowing the snap count.
2. Know what you are going to do with your feet on the first step and maintain correct position of your head. For every block you make, you should have an answer to these two questions: Where is my first step? Where does my head go? Take a controlled first step to maintain balance and power. A short timing step followed by short driving steps is a good technique.
3. Hit with as much power and pop as possible.
4. Once contact is made, sustain it. Follow through and maintain contact with leg drive.
5. Keep the feet spread to insure a good base and keep the feet chopping—when the feet stop, the block stops.
6. Keep your head up and your eyes open.

I found it a lot easier blocking in a game rather than in practice. The defensive men have it a lot tougher in a game because they have a lot of things to watch for and receivers have a better chance to get to them. Other things your players should ask themselves: What split is needed? Which foot should I push off of? Where should my eyes look? Which stunt should I be alert for? Am I high on my block?

DOWNFIELD BLOCKING

There are several reasons why tight ends must be effective downfield blockers, but these reasons all add up to winning. No tight end can be very effective if he is only involved in the offense when there is a pass play called or a running play called to his side of the line. He must be involved and contribute to every play that occurs while he is on the field. Following are some rules that are fundamental for effective downfield blocking:

1. When you leave the huddle you must believe that this play is going to be the one that will break into the secondary, and that your block will be the one to spring the ball carrier for extra yards or the score.

2. Come off of the line fast. The defensive man should not be able to tell any difference between a run and a pass by your release.

3. The approach angle you take to your man will depend on the probable path of the ball carrier.

4. Get your eyes on your man. His eyes and face will tell you when the ball carrier is behind you. Don't peek at your ball carrier and lose your man.

5. You are blocking against the most agile and quick people on the defensive unit. Your timing is most important. If you attack at the same time the ball carrier is there, your block will have the maximum effect. Hitting too early and allowing the defender to recover is just as bad as hitting too late. Keep your head up and don't clip. Try to time the block so that you attack your man as the ball carrier arrives. Sustain your block as long as you can, stay after the man. Your final effort, your final nudge, may just get enough of the defender to allow the ball carrier to break free for the long gain or the touchdown.

Coach your tight ends to have pride in being complete players. They have areas to excel in and they should spend good practice time on each area every day—blocking in the line, blocking downfield, receiving, and running with the ball.

Coaching the Running Back as Receiver

5

CHARACTERISTICS OF THE POSITION

The running back is the focal point of any offense. If a team does not have a good running attack it will be difficult for them to have a consistently successful passing attack. The running game rests on the shoulders of the running backs. They must be able to take advantage of blocking in the line, and find holes to run through that are not where they were designed to be. They must be capable of blocking for the other backs as well. More and more frequently in modern football, they are asked to be threats to the defense as pass receivers, too.

The idea of throwing to running backs is not new and it is very sound. It makes very good sense to get the ball to the player who has the most experience at running with it. A good passing offense will include the possibility of getting the ball to the backs. As a rule, the running back is not usually the best receiver on the team. Because of his alignment, most of the time he is not the threat to the secondary that the wide receiver or the tight end is. But with a few well-executed patterns, the running back can attack the defense where it is most vulnerable to the pass.

The running back can be used to create flooded areas for the secondary to contend with; he can be isolated one-on-one with a linebacker; he can cause the secondary to rotate or spread in a fashion the opponents don't want; and with motion, he can be used to eliminate double coverage on a wide receiver. The contribution of the running back to the passing game is no longer just that of a safety valve receiver for a troubled quarterback.

Because of the way many practices are scheduled, the running back usually concentrates on the skills necessary for the success of the running game. Many times this will cause him to be less skilled as a receiver. If you anticipate utilizing your running backs as receivers in the passing game, they must be allowed to practice the necessary skills. Running backs must put in a lot of time with the quarterbacks working on patterns that will be called in game situations. Just like the wide receivers and tight ends, they must work on the variety of catches they will be faced with in ball games. Your backs must realize that being a skilled receiver is necessary if they are to become complete backs in a balanced offense.

The practice schedule will be covered in greater detail in Chapter Seven, however, one point needs to be made at this time. If the offensive philosophy is to throw nearly half of the time, then the quarterback and the receiver should spend nearly half of their practice time on the passing game. And it follows that if the running back is expected to catch 10 to 15 percent of the passes thrown, for example, then he should be scheduled to practice the passing game 10 to 15 percent of the time.

The characteristics of the running back are, for the most part, excellent in relation to the passing game. He can usually get into his pattern with relative ease, he frequently knows who is going to be covering him in a certain pattern from the scouting report, and he usually matches up very well physically with either linebackers or defensive backs. Because of his speed, he is seldom at a disadvantage versus a defensive back. The skills that make him efficient as a runner who carries the ball frequently during a game also contribute to his ability as a receiver. Since he is a skilled runner, it is sound philosophy to want to get the football to him and match him against a defender in the open field after he receives the ball. For this reason it is not necessary for the running back to work on many deep pass patterns, since he should have success receiving the ball in an open area and be allowed to utilize his running ability to make yardage. This reduces the number of pass-receiving skills he must master, yet still makes him an offensive dimension that the defense must prepare for and be ready to stop.

Although the running back is not usually the best receiver on the team, that does not exclude the possibility of the back being one of the leading receivers on the team. Offensively, on all levels of participation, you must take advantage of what the defense gives.

The zone defense and double coverages, as well as other tactics that are commonplace in the pro leagues, are becoming more and more widespread in college and high school football. Since the running back can be utilized in so many ways to help the success of the passing game, it is essential that he be well prepared.

The Halfback Cross Route

Before the snap, the halfback should check the alignment of the defense. He needs to locate the man whom it is his responsibility to block. If he blitzes or rushes the passer, then the halfback has to step up and take him on. His technique is to stay in the middle of the defender with his butt aimed at the passer. He has to keep the defensive man off of the quarterback. Another technique is to hit and recoil just like offensive linemen are taught to do. As a last resort, he may have to cut or chop a rushing defender. This is not effective very often, and not at all against a defender who is under control in his rush. Caution your halfbacks against using one of these techniques exclusively; they must be able to execute all of them.

If the defender, whom the halfback is responsible for, does not rush the passer or blitz, then the halfback should release quickly out of the backfield and drive upfield to a depth of 5 yards. He should plant his outside foot and break squarely across the middle. This is a combination route for the halfback and the slot, so it is important that the halfback stay 5 to 6 yards deep. The slot back is at 15 yards and there needs to be 10 yards distance between the two receivers. Instruct your halfbacks that in this pattern they should run away from man-to-man coverage, and they should run underneath the linebackers if the defense is deployed in zone coverage as illustrated in Figures 5-1 and 5-2.

The Catch: Drills that will help prepare your halfback for this type of catch in a game situation are

High Look-In	High Behind
Low Ball	Behind
Concentration	Holler Ball
One Hand	

The Slot Back: Should be split from the tackle about 5 yards. He must release off of the line quickly and go outside any defender trying to hold him up (so that he will not collide with the defensive man). His pattern calls for him to run to a depth of 13 to 15 yards and then to break across the middle. Instruct your slot backs to run away from man-to-man coverage and to run over the top of the linebackers if there is a zone coverage.

The Split End: Executes a sideline route at a depth of 15 to 16 yards. Maintains width, and on the break he should come back away from the defensive man.

The Tight End: Needs to release from the line of scrimmage with the fastest method available—either inside or outside. His route is the "Deep Post." He must be a quick threat to the deep middle area and force the defense to honor him.

The Fullback: His responsibilities are nearly identical to those of the halfback. He checks the defensive alignment to pick up his key. If his key rushes the passer or comes on a blitz, then he has to take him. If he doesn't blitz, he should release out of the backfield quickly and drive upfield to a depth of 5 yards, plant his inside foot and break outside.

The Quarterback: Executes a straight drop back. He must get back quickly and set up at about 9 yards deep. He first keys both safeties as he is dropping back to determine the type of coverage being utilized by the defense. If there is a blitz, his backs will not be in patterns so he will have to look to the split end, slot, or the tight end—whoever has the best chance for a completion due to the abilities of the receiver and the abilities of the defensive man covering the receiver. If there is no blitz, the quarterback should think halfback or slot versus zone coverage. If the underneath defenders, the linebackers, drop deep, he should hit the halfback. If the linebackers are influenced to stay up on the halfback, he should drop the ball over the linebackers to the slot. Occasionally the quarterback should throw deep to the tight end to keep the weak safety honest. In various man-to-man coverage, your halfback and slot—as well as the split end, fullback, and tight end—are matched up against individuals. Your game plan each week may vary according to the team you are playing and the type of pass coverages they like to use. You could go into a game planning to feature any one of the five receivers in this pattern.

The Fullback Cross Route or
The Halfback Out Route

In this route the same rules for the pickup of blitzes are in effect. Check the keys first; run the pattern second. If a blitz, the halfback must take his man. If there is no blitz, then the halfback should release with speed, drive upfield to a

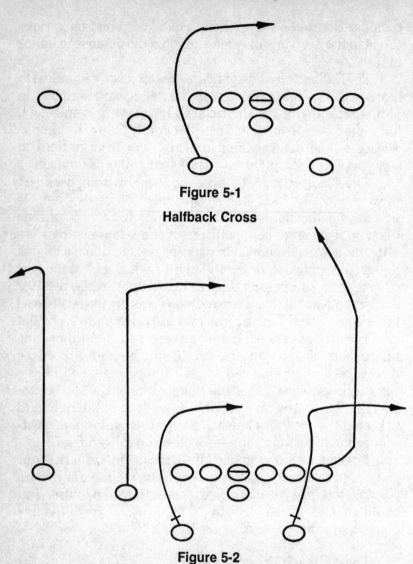

Figure 5-1

Halfback Cross

Figure 5-2

Pattern with Halfback Cross

depth of 5 yards, plant his *inside* foot and break to the outside.
If the defense is in man-to-man coverage, the halfback must
fight for outside position and stay on his route. He should try
to force the defensive man to move backward or to the inside
before he makes his break. A good inside fake might be used

so that the defender thinks that the halfback is trying to run a "Halfback Cross" route. Again, the halfback runs away with speed from man coverage to the outside. If the defense is in a zone, he should stay at a depth of 5 to 6 yards. See Figures 5-3 and 5-4.

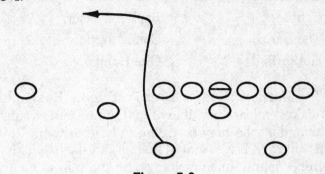

Figure 5-3

Halfback Out

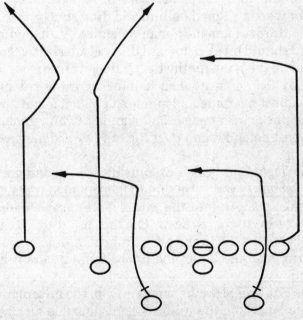

Figure 5-4

Pattern with Halfback Out

The Catch: Catching drills that will help the receivers prepare for this catch in game conditions are

High Back to Passer	High Behind
Low Ball	Scoop
Behind	Back to Passer
Toe Dance	Concentration
Holler Ball	One Hand

The Slot Back: Runs a "Deep Post" route. He should take the quickest release possible off of the line and escape from any defender who may be trying to hold him up. This is a speed route and it is essential that he gets deep quickly. If he recognizes man-to-man coverage, he should put a move on the defender covering him and then break for the post area.

The Split End: His pattern is the "Deep Flag." He should drive upfield to a depth of about 9 yards against a zone defender who is aligned on him and dropping back to cover the deep third, or a man-to-man defender. At that point, the split end should break in toward the post area for two to three steps before breaking for the flag. If the receiver recognizes a roll-up by the defense when he breaks for the sideline, he should adjust his route and aim for a point at about 18 yards from the line of scrimmage. This should put him underneath the deepest defender and over the top of the defensive man rolling up.

The Tight End: Takes an outside release and goes to a depth of about 14 yards. He should then plant his outside foot and break squarely into the middle. He must be aware of staying 14 to 16 yards deep. On this route the tight end should be instructed to run away from man-to-man coverage and to run over the top of the linebackers if there is a zone coverage.

The Fullback: Has the same rules for the blitz pick-up. If the defender whom the fullback is responsible for does not come for the passer, then the fullback releases quickly out of the backfield and drives upfield to a depth of 5 yards. He should break inside off of his outside foot, breaking squarely across the middle.

This is a combination route for the fullback and the tight end, so it is very important for the fullback to stay at his depth of 5 yards. The tight end will be about 16 yards deep and the 10 to 11 yards distance between the receivers is necessary for the success of this route. The fullback needs to understand that he is to run away from man-to-man coverage, and to stay underneath the linebackers if the defense is in zone coverage.

The Quarterback: Can feature either side of this pattern, depending upon the team he is facing and the pass coverage they employ. Against some teams he can be instructed to think of the halfback as the number one receiver versus a two-deep secondary with a roll-up on the split end. He should look to the halfback first, then the split end, before looking to the tight end and fullback side. Against the same coverage, he could look to the fullback and tight end first before going to the halfback and split end side. This strategy could also be affected by the knowledge of your players and their abilities as compared to the defense and the defenders.

Your quarterback should drop straight back to a depth of 9 yards while reading both safeties. If there is a blitz, he should think slot back, tight end, or split end. If there is no blitz he should pick a side as discussed above. He can be instructed to look for the halfback first, but if the halfback is not open he should go directly to the fullback-tight end combination as his second choice.

If he selects, or if the game plan determines, that he look to the fullback-tight end combination first, and the defense aligns in a zone, he should look to the fullback first if the underneath coverage is dropping deep and ignore the fullback. If the underneath defenders have been influenced up on the fullback, then he should hit the tight end by dropping the ball over the underneath coverage or throwing the ball between them. You may have to instruct your quarterback to throw to the slot back on the post occasionally to keep the deep middle defender concerned with his area. If faced with man coverages, each receiver has a good chance of being open. The game plan for that particular opponent will help determine who to feature in the particular case. Again, review Figures 5-3 and 5-4 for this route.

The Halfback Hook Route

Again, both backs have the same rules for picking up the blitz: check keys first, run the pattern second. If the halfback's man blitzes, then the halfback must block him. When he reads no blitz, he releases with speed and drives upfield to a depth of 6 yards. He should plant his inside foot and turn to the outside and hook. Instruct him to turn to the outside to draw the linebacker coverage out, thus opening up the lane between them for the split end.

The halfback must get his head around quickly and look for the ball. He needs to get his feet under him, spread slightly with his weight on the balls of his feet, ready to react if the ball is thrown off target. If the defense is in man coverage, the halfback should maneuver a little away from the defender (much like separating from a defender in basketball). This distance cannot be too great or the quarterback will have difficulty making an accurate throw because the receiver will not be where the quarterback expects him to be. Under no circumstances should the halfback lead his defender into the middle.

Coaching Point: Figures 5-5 and 5-6 illustrate the running backs turning to the outside on the "Halfback Hook" route. You want your backs to hook to the outside to draw the linebacker coverage to the outside in order to open up the split end. If the linebackers or underneath defenders ignore the back, the quarterback should be coached to deliver the ball to the halfback.

The Catch: The following drills should help the halfback prepare for the catch on the "Halfback Hook" route:

High Hook   Scoop

Concentration   Holler Ball

One Hand

The Wingback (Flanker): Releases quickly on the "Deep Post" route. He should always be conscious of the safety in the deep middle. If the safety is careless about his coverage, the receiver should alert you, the coach. (He needs to be able to recognize whether the safety is reacting up *as* the quarterback throws the ball or if he is starting to gamble and is reacting up *before* the quarterback releases the ball to the split end or the backs.) If the wingback is being covered man-to-man he may have to vary his approaches to beat the defender. He may try to make a good outside fake, or run at the defender's inside to get inside position on him before breaking to the post. While the receiver should be able to execute either of these moves, he should have a good idea of which approach will be more successful before the game from checking the scouting report and studying game films.

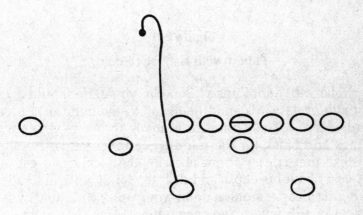

Figure 5-5

Halfback Hook

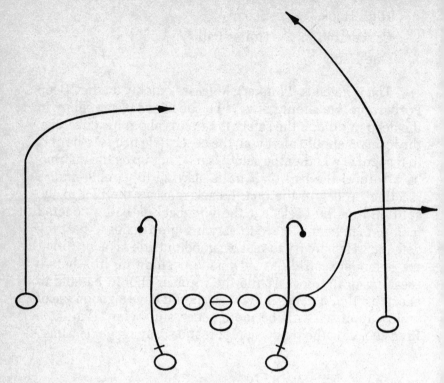

Figure 5-6

Pattern with Halfback Hook

The Split End: Runs a "Bend In" route. He should drive upfield for 11 yards and "Bend In" to the middle 15 to 18 yards deep. A common error of many receivers is to hurry things and break for the middle before 11 yards. Another mistake that is easy to make is for the receiver to get too careless about his depth and drift too far downfield to 20 or 25 yards deep. Impress upon your split ends that when executing this pattern, no deeper than 18, no shorter than 15 is the rule.

If there is man-to-man coverage, try to get inside position on the defender (if the receiver can get the inside position before his break, when he bends to the middle, he will leave the defender on the outside). He should run with speed away from man coverage. Against zone coverages, he should just get his proper depth.

The Fullback: has the same rules for picking up a blitz. When there is no blitz, the fullback releases quickly and drives upfield to a depth of 6 yards just as the halfback does. He should plant his inside foot and turn to the outside to widen the area between the linebackers for the split end. As he turns to the outside, he will hook. He must turn to the outside.

The fullback has to turn his head around quickly and look for the ball. He needs to get his feet under him, spread slightly, with his weight on the balls of his feet ready to react to the ball. Versus man-to-man coverage, the fullback should work to separate himself from the defender just as the halfback should without taking his man into the middle.

The Quarterback: Should take a straight drop back to a depth of 9 yards. As he drops he should read both safeties to determine the type of coverage the defense is in. If the defense is blitzing, his backs will not be out and he should think wingback, tight end, or split end. If there is no blitz, he should think halfback or split end first. Against zone coverages, if the linebacker or the defender responsible for the underneath coverage in the area the halfback releases into drops deep, the quarterback should throw to the halfback. If the defender is influenced up by the halfback, then the quarterback should throw to the split end. The halfback and the fullback are deployed in an attempt to open up a throwing lane to the split end. If the backs are obviously being ignored by the defense, your quarterback should keep throwing to them and picking up the shorter gains. With practice your quarterback will get the knack of hitting the split end on the "Bend In" between the underneath defenders. He will occasionally have to throw to the wingback deep to keep the deep safety honest. Review Figures 5-5 and 5-6 for this play.

THE RUNNING BACK AS A DEEP THREAT

There is no discussion in this book of pass patterns that include the running backs as receivers in the deeper areas of the defense. This is not to imply that your running backs cannot be successfully utilized as deep receivers. As was stated in Chapter Two, "Catching the long ball is the most advanced part of the receiver's art." This being the case, it would require a great deal more practice for a running back to be a consistent deep pass receiver as well as a major part of the rushing offense. For the most part, the demands made upon the running back in the rushing offense require the greatest portion of his practice time.

Although execution of the actual pass route would not be that difficult (pass protection breaking down could be a concern), the timing and coordination necessary would not be as accomplished as it would be between the quarterback and the receiver who had run the route repeatedly with the passer in practice. Such a loss of timing could mean the difference between a percentage pass and a ball thrown up for grabs.

The practiced execution of the running back patterns included in this chapter will enable your pass offense to attack zone and man-to-man coverages in areas weakened by the defensive alignments themselves, by inadequate personnel, or by the routes of the other receivers and the defensive reaction to those routes. Occasionally, your quarterback may need to be reminded to take advantage of what the defense is giving, and frequently, that will be the running back out of the backfield into a short area.

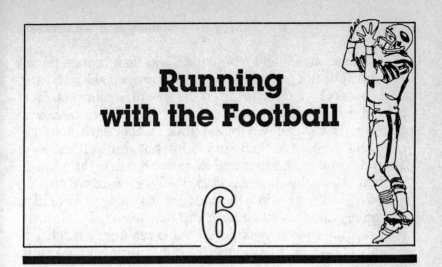

Running with the Football

6

GOOD RECEIVERS CAN BE DEVELOPED
INTO GOOD BALL CARRIERS

A receiver gets limited opportunities to run with the ball. The majority of the time, the defenders close in on him so quickly after a catch that he is usually tackled almost immediately with no chance of getting away. If he gets one or two opportunities a game to have some running room, that is above average.

Because he does have so few chances to run with the ball, I think it is really important that a receiver gets in the habit *during practice* of exploding after the catch and striving to run at full speed. I mean cutting and maneuvering, stopping and starting, and then sprinting with the ball held under his arm properly. It doesn't make any difference if there are defenders there or not. Just acting like there are defenders there will help him develop his ball carrying technique so that in a game he will automatically and instinctively react. We play like we practice.

One of the most valuable things I ever did as a player was to study good runners in game films, diagram their various maneuvers and techniques, and then imitate them. For example, in a game film I see a ball carrier make a 50-yard run. He fakes a tackler just past the line of scrimmage, cuts behind a blocker, sets up a defender with a step fake and turns on the speed down the sideline. Further downfield, he cuts back across the field, and is hit, but spins all the way around, keeps his balance and extends his arm to the ground to help regain his balance completely, then turns on the speed again and goes into the end zone. I would put a run like this on my Ball Carrying Sheet, and have a mental picture of it in my mind of me making the same run after a catch.

By collecting a few runs like this, a receiver (or a running back) can really develop his running ability more nearly to its full potential. I used to work on this primarily when working by myself in the off season getting back into condition. As I went from one run to another I could almost hear the crowd of 60,000 people cheering me on. It was one of the greatest conditioning drills I ever did. Between each run I would pause to recover my wind, and then go again. I re-enacted the run just as I'd seen it on film.

Running with the ball like this allows your players to condition themselves with a minimum of boredom. It also lets them add a little imagination to their drills. Imagination, or dreaming, if you will, is where self-motivation begins; and players who are self-motivated are the best kind to work with.

POINTS OF EMPHASIS FOR THE BALL CARRIER

In running with the ball after the catch, your receivers should remember the most important thing is to keep a tight grip on the ball—to keep it in close to the body, protecting it. This is essential for *all* receivers to remember.

The tight end can run into more traffic than a wide receiver, and due to his strength he may be harder to bring down. Coach your tight ends to cover the ball with both hands whenever they are surrounded and in a crowd. Even when struggling to break out of the grasp of a tackler, they must maintain the tight, protecting grip on the football.

The next thing for your receivers to remember is to be concerned about speed when carrying the ball. Speed and explosion after the catch are essential. They must get going, take off for that goal line. While emphasizing the things to do when running with the football, it is frequently necessary to remind them not to run with the ball *before* it is caught and securely tucked away. Seeing some open room will sometimes cause a receiver to take his eyes off of the ball in his eagerness to start running.

In the process of catching the ball the receiver will actually lose some speed. Very few passes allow a receiver to catch the ball without breaking stride. Consequently, the defender is closing the gap on the receiver. He has to explode as soon as he makes the catch and turn upfield after he has the ball securely in his possession. You must emphasize to the receivers to get going, to attain full speed. As your receiver catches the ball, he must put the ball away—watch it in and tuck it away—and then explode. He should work on these things every time he catches a football.

RESULTS TO EXPECT FROM PRACTICING BALL CARRYING

Running with the ball was always a great thrill. Every receiver sooner or later will get the chance to be a ball carrier. You can help your receivers develop their ability now and help them be prepared to take advantage of the one or two opportunities a game that may come their way. The following improvements should result from the practice of carrying the ball:

1. Improved balance
2. Improved awareness of tacklers while running at full speed and cutting
3. The ability to use fakes and evasive maneuvers

4. The ability to quickly regain top speed after stopping or dodging a tackler

5. The ability to keep the ball held tightly throughout the run

6. The ability to simply run full speed with a football under the arm and maintain control

7. Most importantly, the instinct of *exploding* with the ball after the catch

INCREASING SPEED

I believe that every athlete has a "speed potential" or a "speed ceiling." There is a limit to how fast an athlete can run a 100-yard dash, for example, no matter how much work he does to improve his speed. This you could call a "ceiling." I firmly believe that there are many athletes who operate *below* their speed potential. I hope some of the following information will help your athletes get the most out of their ability to simply run.

Running track while I was in college was probably the most important thing I did as a college athlete. The main reason I worked on track was to be a better football player. Our track coach, McAdoo Keaton, gave me a lot of tips and let me work with the sprinters. He taught me to run with my upper body relaxed. He stressed relaxation of the face, neck, shoulders and hands while sprinting at full speed.

Our routine (which could be included in pre-season and early season practices) was to first warm up and stretch. Second, we would run a couple of straightaways for form, gradually increasing speed and stretching out the stride, but remaining controlled. Third, after we were good and loose and warmed up, but still fresh, we did out starts—10s, 15s, 20s, and 40s; fourth, a lot of straightaways, walking the curves on the 440 track. As we started into the straightaway, we would start running at a controlled speed, stressing form—toes pointed ahead, good knee lift, reaching out with long strides, power stroke or bounce off of the ball of the foot (not flat-footed), and upper body relaxation. We would gradually increase the speed, then hit top speed and hold it. Finally, we would slow down at the end of the straightaway before walking around the curve and recovering our wind. These are called "build-ups," "accelerations," or "booms." Repeat the procedure into the next straightaway. Several repetitions are done at a time.

As a result of doing this routine for four years, I developed the proper running form, relaxation, strength, endurance, and more speed. Confidence increased as I began to compete with the sprinters. I also believe this caused my legs to develop, since this took place during a period of growth. This running form became habit—a part of me, automatic. It paid off well for me in football. A pass receiver needs all the speed he can get, plus a relaxed upper body as he catches the football.

There can be little doubt that most athletes can improve their running form and starting ability. Many college and professional coaching staffs spend time and put emphasis on teaching their players tips on running. They also encourage them to learn from college track coaches during the off season. Several outstanding college athletes have dramatically improved their 40-yard times as a result of this work and emphasis.

There is one tip on improving speed that any football player can do everyday in practice: *Run full speed* while practicing or playing football. I've seen players (and have experienced this myself) get into the habit of running at a controlled speed so much that they lose their ability to go at top speed.

SOME METHODS FOR INCREASING SPEED

Bobby Mitchell had an outstanding college career at Illinois and an equally outstanding professional career with the Cleveland Browns and the Washington Redskins. He was noted for his speed, quickness, and quick explosion. He shared his experiences on developing speed with me. Bobby said that when he went to Illinois as a freshman he could run the 100-yard dash in 9.8 seconds. Due to the encouragement of the coach, he went out for track to run the 220-yard low hurdles. He had never run this event before. In six months' time of practice and competition, his speed improved in the 100-yard dash from 9.8 to 9.4. Most would agree that this represents a dramatic improvement. How did Bobby account for such improvement?

This is how he explains it. Because of the demands of running a race like the low hurdles, he was required to develop more strength and endurance. He also pointed out that he had to develop an even stride so that his steps between the hurdles would not vary. Most important, his stride *lengthened*. In other words, he began to cover more ground per step than he did previously. Bobby thinks this was due primarily to more flexibility in his hips and hamstring muscles. This flexibility was developed by the repeated hurdling motion.

"Jumping to get over a hurdle and then immediately accelerating for the next hurdle also caused me to develop *explosion* power. This really was noticeable in football when I carried the ball the next year," he said. His balance and agility was greatly aided as well.

There is no doubt that Bobby Mitchell was blessed with great natural speed, but he may never have attained his *full speed potential* without working as he did in track.

There is a similar method of making a player's running stride consistent and then lengthening it without utilizing hurdles, which can be done in season or off season nearly anywhere. First, measure several parallel running lanes and mark them in varying lengths so that the athletes can step on the marks while running the lanes to insure consistent strides. When an athlete can consistently and easily hit the marks while running full speed, then he should move to the lane marked in the next length of strides and work on that lane until he can hit the marks consistently while running at full speed again.

As long as he can move to a longer stride, hit the marks, run in a relaxed manner, and increase his speed, keep him moving. When he has to overstride, or if his speed drops, or if he cannot run relaxed, then he should move back down one length. For example, an athlete can run 40 yards hitting strides marked in 6-foot lengths in 4.9 seconds. He moves to the lane marked off in 6½ foot lengths and after several days can hit every mark and is timed in 4.8 seconds. But when he moves to the lane marked in 7 foot lengths he cannot relax and hit the marks and his time drops to 5.1 seconds. If this happens, then he should move back to 6½ foot strides and continue to work on his form.

The method just described is not guaranteed to make every player on your squad a 4.5 burner, but it should help the athletes who have an inconsistent stride to smooth out and thus run faster. Many others will benefit just from concentrating on form and consistency. A few runners tend to overstride in an attempt to run faster and they can see an improvement by shortening their strides and being able to relax.

As coaches, all of us are expected to demonstrate results with the material we have to work with. Some of us have only top athletes while others have average and often below-average players. Regardless of the raw talent that we are blessed with or that we lack, a very important and fundamental aspect of our profession is to take what we have and help our players develop to their fullest potential. Sometimes the most important thing we can help a young man learn is how to work hard to improve himself in fundamental areas of his sport. Some of these areas are speed, strength, and agility— areas where *most* athletes can improve and can come nearer to achieving their full potential.

INCREASING LEG STRENGTH

Another factor that is frequently mentioned whenever the subject of speed is discussed is that of increasing leg strength. Many knowledgeable coaches agree that if you can increase an athlete's strength in his legs you can increase his speed. Here are a few approaches to building additional leg strength:

1. Jumping rope
2. Running against resistance, such as an Exer-Genie
3. Running up hills or slopes forward, sideways, and backwards
4. Hiking in plowed fields
5. Running stairs

Coach Ralph Reynolds of Thomas Jefferson High School in Dallas, Texas outlined for me the program that he utilized, which is one of the best I've seen. They combine a lot of starts and running with a weight program designed for the legs. They do leg curls, leg extensions, leg presses, half squats, toe raises, and the rail. At one stage of their program their players will run ten 10s, ten 20s, ten 40s, seven 100s, and five 220s. On their starts they stress lean, short steps, elbows in by the sides and maintaining some forward lean as they accelerate.

A variation of an old exercise is being utilized in many programs to improve athletes in several areas of their development and conditioning. This exercise is the squat thrust. Needing no equipment, it is an excellent method of warm-up (cardiovascular work), and a good strength exercise because it conditions the muscles that enable an athlete to explode off of the line and into a tackle. It is a very good agility type exercise to help increase quickness. Very simply, the athlete assumes a break down position, quickly drops his hands to the ground while keeping his head up, and then kicks his feet straight out behind him and immediately brings them back up underneath him and explodes up to the break down position again. These give the best results when done in sets of 10 for example, building up to 40 or 50 sets during a practice.

By combining work and concentration on the areas of stride, relaxation, and leg strength, athletes should see improvement in their running. These improvements should be noticeable in such things as smoothness, consistency, and speed. It has often been said that if an athlete cannot run, he cannot play. By enabling athletes to learn to run better, faster, and easier, we help them become more confident football players.

Putting
It All Together–
The Practice Schedule

7

HOW I UTILIZE THE MATERIAL ON THE
COLLEGE AND PROFESSIONAL LEVELS

When Playing

The drills for catching the football were used every day. I tried to catch some of each drill every time I was on the practice field. I worked on the moves in every practice also, attempting to perfect the "steps" so the execution during a game was consistent and precise to the detail. Without the multiple moves, getting open would have been impossible during the last six or seven years of my career. The ball-carrying and conditioning drill was a regular part of preparing for the season in April, May, June, as were all the conditioning programs outlined (See Chapter 8).

I knew none of this as a college player and therefore, I didn't use these drills. Only after I became a professional did I utilize them.

In Coaching

The drills for catching are used all through the season. The coaching points on the moves are still used in teaching receivers to run routes. Use of step counting is introduced as a teaching/learning tool. Knowledge of his steps on many routes can help any receiver learn how to run more consistent and efficient pass routes. Some use this tool more than others, depending on background, stride, and running style. It becomes a part of the receiver's repertoire of techniques to get open. The material on conditioning is given to the players every year for their off-season work. All of the material in the book is a part of the year-long coaching process still used.

WARM UP

Stretching

Whether your receivers warm up in a group or as a part of the whole squad, they have to stretch in order to get properly warmed up. The past few years have seen quite a shift in emphasis from calisthenics to stretching exercises as the desired method of warming up. This shift came about mainly as a means to help prevent muscle pulls and other injuries, that were not results of contact.

The proper method of warming up is to slowly and thoroughly stretch the major muscle groups as well as the smaller muscles. I try to teach and warn my receivers about the danger signals muscles give us—tightening up, aching, slightly throbbing. I insist that my players tell me the instant they get a warning signal. The best way to treat a muscle displaying warning symptoms is to quit right then. In practically every case, a receiver will only miss one day. Once the muscle is pulled, it can take anywhere from a week to two weeks to heal. Prevention is the best approach.

Jogging and Easy Running

An additional aspect to warming up is to jog and do some easy running before going full speed in starts, sprints, or routes. This is frequently accomplished by form running after stretching. In addition to making the athlete concentrate on his running form, it also finishes what the stretching exercises have begun. All of your receivers should be able to tell from the way their muscles feel when they have properly warmed up and are ready to go full speed. Whatever methods or sequences you utilize in practice should be utilized when warming up for the actual game. This insures a complete warm up when the athlete may be too nervous to pay much attention to his warm up. A familiar routine helps him physically and has a calming effect on him at the same time.

Catching

Just as the major muscles and the smaller muscle groups have to be properly warmed up, so do the hands and fingers of your receivers. To a receiver a jammed finger or thumb can be as much of a hindrance as a muscle pull. For this reason, your receivers should play some easy catch as a part of their loosening-up routine. After catching a few passes that are easily thrown, they are ready to catch whatever the quarterback or the coach presents to them.

Like the stretching and running, the catching should be done in a set routine before games as well as before every practice. In addition to completing the warm-up process, it bolsters a receiver's confidence to catch the first few passes thrown to him.

INDIVIDUAL DRILLS

Catching Drills

The catching drills described in Chapter Two should be a part of every practice. After you determine some of the strengths and weaknesses of your individual receivers, you can individualize the drills they are to work on in a given practice.

Step Counting

There are many reasons for teaching your receivers to count steps to their routes. Some of the more obvious ones are to develop the consistency and timing between the receiver and the quarterback, and the smoothness achieved by running the route the same way repeatedly. An additional reason that can be especially valuable with your younger receivers is the confidence and reassurance they get from knowing exactly when they are going to cut, fake, and when the ball will be delivered.

After the routes are learned, the receiver may not have to rely on the counting, but it is comforting to always have the steps to fall back on against a particularly tough defender, or when the receiver is facing a clutch situation and the timing is critical.

Maintain Strengths

A receiver may not use the step counting method in a route he has a particular strength in running. Every receiver should be encouraged to develop a strength area such as speed, leaping ability, cutting smoothness, feel for the sidelines, good hands and so on. When a receiver has developed a strength area, he may want to use that strength on certain patterns or against particular defenders or defenses. His confidence will increase when he is sure he can outrun, outleap, or get his body into position versus a certain defender or defense. When he is confident he can do that, he can rely on his strength to get into position and then concentrate on making the catch.

Improve Weaknesses

Just as every receiver should cultivate strengths, nearly every receiver will have one or more areas in which he is not proficient. He should spend at least as much time in practice on these areas as he does on his strengths. By concentrating and striving to improve his weaknesses, he will improve overall and eventually turn weaknesses into strengths. No receiver should ever be satisfied with his ability or his skills. He should always set new goals and look for areas he can improve himself in.

ROUTES WITH THE QUARTERBACK

Individual Routes with No Defense

Every practice, particularly those early in the season, should allow the receiver to run his routes with the quarterback throwing to him for the sole purpose of establishing timing and coordination. This is a low-pressure situation that allows the receiver to execute his route and then concentrate on the catch. This needs to be repeated often enough to allow the two players to establish a sense of timing and coordination between each other, and lets them build confidence in each other.

Individual Routes Versus Man Coverage

As the quarterback and the receiver establish the timing and coordination essential to the successful execution of the pass routes, you can introduce man-to-man coverage for the receiver to run against. After the defender is added it is likely that there will be more dropped passes as the receiver concentrates on the defender more than the ball. As he becomes used to the defender as a part of the route, he will catch more passes.

When facing man-to-man coverages your receivers should be aware of the key points necessary in getting themselves open. The receiver has the advantage in knowing where and when he is going to make his cut while the defender can only react. The receiver has to explode out of the break and look for the ball. Once he picks it up in flight he must not concentrate on anything else but the football. If he has run his route correctly his body will be in the proper relation to the defender and all that remains is to watch it in and tuck it away just as he has done so often in front of the net.

Individual Routes Versus Zone Coverage

Again, execution is the key when running into zone coverage. In addition, your receiver should learn to recognize where his coverage is coming from. This will indicate to him if he is going to open up early in the route, or late, or not at all. Unless expressly directed to do so by you, he should never deviate from his called route. If it becomes apparent to him that the passing lane is closed and he is covered, then his objective becomes not to catch the ball, but to occupy the defenders assigned to cover the zones he enters and keep them from helping the defender into whose zone the ball will be thrown. He is never out of the play; he is always involved.

PATTERNS WITH THE QUARTERBACK

Skeleton Versus Man Coverage

It is sometimes a big adjustment for a receiver to execute his routes correctly when there is a chance he will not have the ball thrown to him. A prime objective of skeleton pass coverage for the receivers is to give them sufficient practice at running their routes whether they are the primary receiver or not. Consistency is a must to keep the defenders playing honestly and to keep from tipping the play or the intended receiver. A receiver who goes at full speed only when he is the intended receiver is a liability to the offensive unit. A defensive back keying such a receiver then knows who is a prime receiver when he releases from the line of scrimmage. The rest of the time, that defender is nearly free to help out in other areas where he could not under normal conditions.

Another valuable lesson to be learned from skeleton pass defense is where to set up after the ball has been thrown to another receiver in order to be in the best position to deliver the block to spring him free after the catch is made. This is a part of the receiver's art that should not be neglected in practice.

Skeleton Versus Zone Coverage

An important skill to be learned in practice is identifying zone coverage as well as where the coverage is coming from. While this is somewhat easier to determine when there is only one receiver in the pattern, it becomes more difficult against a full secondary. It is, however, an essential skill. A receiver should be able to tell who is going to be covering him and where, in all probability, the pass is going to be delivered. As with skeleton pass offense against man coverage, receivers should also know where to set up to be in the best position to deliver the block that may spring the ball carrier into the open after he has made the catch.

The value of the quarterback's throwing against both skeleton situations is important if he is going to learn where certain zone coverages are likely to be vulnerable to specific patterns, and where his receivers are more likely to become open against the various man coverages.

Reading the Defense

Just as the quarterback reads a certain key or keys as he is setting up, the receiver has keys to read on some patterns to tell him if he is to break the route into a specific area or to run away from the coverage. Your receivers should know which keys to read and what you expect them to know from the different reactions of the key. True coordination between the quarterback and his receivers occurs when they read the same thing and they are in a situation where they know before the pass is thrown to whom it will be thrown. They can then occupy their defenders and set themselves up to block for the ball carrier. This knowledge can be invaluable against a defensive secondary that may possess greater speed than the corps of receivers. Good execution, combined with the ability to read the defense, is essential and desirable if the offense is going to consistently complete a high percentage of passes against all types of pass defenses.

Basic Reads

There are two things the receiver should look for to determine his read of the defender. The first of these is alignment. Generally, the defender will align himself closer to the receiver if he is playing man coverage. The second thing to look for is where the defender is looking at the snap of the ball. If he is playing zone, he will most likely be keying the quarterback and not concentrating solely on the receiver.

While the quarterback can read different keys and should have a more certain read, the receiver can usually get a very good idea of the scheme of the secondary by reading his defender and knowing what to look for.

RELEASING

Although releasing has been discussed before, it must be an integral part of practices and it must be mastered. The receiver must be able to get out into the route cleanly to maintain the timing and coordination that has been established in practice. This is a fundamental that goes back to the stance. If a defender can tell from your receiver's stance whether he is going into a route or going to block on the line, you have a problem.

One method of correcting such a tipoff is to have your receivers get into their stances and then call the play, much the same as if an automatic had been called at the line. This eliminates, or at least points out, when a receiver has more than one stance depending upon the play. Once this is pointed out to him, he should work on it before and after practice as well as during practice to eliminate it.

When a receiver has mastered a consistent stance and is able to execute the various methods of releasing from the line cleanly, then he will not be knocked off of his route easily or held up at the line of scrimmage. This means that the timing and coordination of the quarterback and the receiver will not be destroyed and the secondary will have to play pass defense honestly and cover the whole field.

BLOCKING TECHNIQUES

Variety

Your receivers should be able to successfully deliver a variety of blocks at the same point of attack whenever they are called upon to do so. For example, a receiver may be assigned to block the defensive back, forcing the corner hard versus an option. In one instance the seal block, setting up in the proper position and letting the defender come to him, may be the preferred block, while against a different cover, the successful block may be a run-through type where the blocker attempts to knock the defender away from the point of attack long enough to allow the ball carrier to clear the area.

If you expect your receivers to be able to execute four different blocks against a defensive back, then they should practice those four types of blocks every day—even if they simply release from the line and set up. If the next opponent is expected to be in a defense that will require only two of the four blocks to be executed correctly, your receivers should still practice all four types. Repetition and consistency are vital to consistent blocking. In addition, your receivers' confidence will increase with the knowledge that they can block a defender in a variety of ways—not just one.

Timing

Frequently, the successful block is the one delivered at the right time, more so than one that knocks a defender off of his feet. If a defender who has been knocked off of his feet has time to recover and still make the tackle, then the block is ineffective. More desirable is the block, even if it is simply a shielding maneuver, which keeps the defender from making contact with the ball carrier.

If you must utilize small receivers to also block for your rushing game, then they should be proficient at timing their blocks and not concerned about knocking people down. If the timing is good, a poor block under different circumstances is often effective. To achieve this timing your receivers have to work on the blocking phase of their game in every practice with the ball carrier in the same relationship to them that he will be in during a game.

It is very important for you, the coach, to emphasize to your receivers the importance of effective blocking. You should encourage your receivers to take pride in their blocking. The running backs should reinforce this by complimenting the receiver who does a good job of blocking. As much as any other phase of football, blocking is a matter of being determined to get the job accomplished.

RUNNING DRILLS

Be Prepared

As discussed in Chapter Six, the receiver will probably have limited opportunities to really break free and run with the ball. When he has the chance he should capitalize on it. To do this he will have to practice running with the ball in practice daily. Initially, have your receivers work on using their strengths and natural talents to break away after the catch is made. If a player is elusive and possesses quick feet but is not very fast, then have him work on using his elusiveness to escape defenders immediately after the catch. He can practice this by making a catch in practice and then breaking upfield while faking to the inside and then cutting for the sideline. After running up the sideline for several yards, he could cut back inside sharply as though eluding a defender who is closing in on him in a good angle of pursuit. The point to emphasize is to encourage your receivers to do what they feel comfortable doing while running with the ball. As long as they maintain possession and move toward the goal line, they should utilize a strength. Whatever you and the receiver decide is best for him to do, he should practice it a few times every practice.

If, on the other hand, you have a receiver who is fast and not particularly shifty, then he should turn upfield and accelerate and never deviate from his course. If he is about to be caught by a defender using a good pursuit angle, he need only give a head fake to the inside to gain a step on the defender and explode straight for the goal line.

Your receivers need to practice running, regaining balance, running through an arm tackle, and attacking a tackler to gain the most yardage possible.

After your receivers have worked on utilizing their strengths to break away for big yardage, then begin to work other maneuvers into their running drills. Physically, this will help you develop receivers who are potential game breakers. Mentally, you will have receivers who believe they can get the big gain, who are confident, and who will work hard in practice to improve their skills so they will not waste one opportunity to run with the ball.

SPECIAL SITUATIONS

A Receiver Breaking Loose

Whenever a receiver sees a teammate breaking loose for a big gain and possible score, he should get involved by getting himself in position to throw a block or cut off a pursuing defender. With experience, your receivers will know when they are not going to get the pass thrown to them. When this is the case, the first thought is to get into position as soon as the pass is caught. With the linemen confined to the line of scrimmage during a dropback or play action pass the only possible help downfield is from the running backs or the other receivers. All complete receivers are aware that their job is not complete just because they have run a pattern or thrown a block. If there is a possibility of gaining further yardage, their job is not finished until the ball is blown dead and they have thrown an extra-effort block.

The Quarterback Scrambling

Your receivers need to practice what to do when the quarterback is chased out of the pocket. If they have seen many televised football games, they have often heard from the usually knowledgeable commentary what a heads-up play it is when a receiver comes back toward the troubled quarterback. If asked off of the field what to do in such a situation they could probably come up with the right answer. Knowing the right answer is not sufficient if the reaction is missing. The only way to insure the proper reaction is to practice the situation. Two or three times during a practice instruct the quarterback to scramble as though rushed from the pocket. After experiencing the actual situation a few times your receivers will react as they should.

You should explain to them exactly what you expect of them. If they are to continue to the middle of the field or to the sideline if the route they were on sent them to those areas, only breaking back toward the quarterback, tell them why. Occasionally have the quarterback pull the ball down after leaving the pocket and run with it. The receivers should see the necessity of coming back to the quarterback to block in such a situation and helping him get out of bounds if that is what you want done. The main point is that they will only react as they have done in practice, not as they have been told to do.

Interception

Whenever the defense intercepts a pass, the receiver must immediately think of his defensive responsibility. The initial reaction should be to alert his teammates of the interception. Next, he should position himself to narrow the field for the defender and limit his running options. Finally, he should attempt to tackle him. Containment should be practiced.

Fumble

A fumble can be just as costly as an interception. Loss of possession combined with the lost chance to score can sometimes be a devastating event. A receiver can be a real hero if he can be around the ball and recover a fumble to retain possession. Whenever this happens it should not be a chance occurrence, instead, it should be by design. You should have your receivers practice not only covering the loose ball, but being in position to do so.

When a running play is called, the receiver to the side of the call should execute his block as planned, and when the ball carrier has passed him he should follow the ball carrier and his progress downfield. If he can get within about five yards of the runner, he will be in very good position in the event of a fumble. Since he will not have a good opportunity to throw a critical block, he can pay more attention and be alert for a fumble.

A receiver can achieve the same relationship to another receiver after a reception for the same reason. If the outside receivers see the pass being completed over the middle, then both of them should converge in the middle to block if they can, or to cover a fumble if necessary. A receiver catching a pass over the middle is separated from the football more frequently than a catch near the sideline. All receivers should be aware of this and react accordingly. This fact should not deter any player from running a route into the middle.

If any or all of the situations mentioned above are important to you as a coach, then they should be practiced frequently—daily or at least weekly. A coach cannot expect a player to react in the heat of the battle as he has been told to verbally. But if the player has practiced the reaction and has reacted properly and successfully in practice, then he can be expected to react appropriately in a game situation. To insure the proper reactions, coaches have to be sure that they have their players practice exactly what they want done. A longtime axiom in football has been, "Have a plan for everything and practice it."

By practicing how to react to many of the situations that frequently occur during games, your team will get more of the "good breaks" during a season, because the breaks don't just happen; they are a result of preparation meeting with opportunity.

Three Goals to Conditioning

THE FIRST GOAL— START THE SEASON IN GAME CONDITION

My rookie year in pro ball was something less than a success. I caught 13 passes while playing in 12 games. Because of this lack of production, my neck was on the chopping block and I knew it. Also because of this situation I learned one of the most important things I have ever learned as an athlete. I wish I had learned it sooner, say, back in high school and college. It would really have made a difference. The lesson I learned was *how to get into condition.*

Motivated by fear, I began to plan how I could best prepare for my second year with the Colts. This was in the off-season during March and April before the reporting date in July. I didn't know very much, but I knew one way to get an advantage on my competition was to be in better shape than they were. I had always heard my dad make the statement that his teams really got into good shape after they had played a game or two. He said that no matter how they were prepared beforehand, they still increased their conditioning level when they were forced to keep going for a full game; to keep going when they were tired. So I decided to play several games before reporting to training camp.

I sent for some game films and from these films I listed each play. I included kickoffs and all phases of the kicking game. The receivers used to be on the kicking teams, too. What it roughly came to was this: There were approximately 70 offensive plays plus the kicking game. These were divided into about six or seven series in the first half totalling about 35 plays, and six or seven series in the second half totalling about 35 plays as well. This was for a 60-minute game, of course.

So I began to run and get myself into shape. After a couple of weeks of conditioning I decided to see how much of a game I could play without running out of gas. I took a sheet of paper out with me that had all the plays listed for all four quarters. I also took a clock onto the field. Then I started the game.

I did my assignment on the kickoff return. I trotted to the "huddle" for my first play on the sheet. Following the order on the sheet, run or pass, I ran the play just like in a game—at full speed. Then, just like in a game, I ran back to the huddle. I paused there for 10 to 12 seconds, then out of the huddle and up to the line. I ran at full speed for the next play. When the series ended, I took a normal between-series break (in a game this would be an average of three to four minutes on the bench). Then I went back for the next series. In that first "game" I found myself tiring badly late in the second quarter. So that was all I did the first time out.

After another week of working out, I played another "game." This time I made it further. In about another week, I went through the complete sheet of plays. I don't remember how many times I went through that procedure in the off-season, but I found out something when I started through two-a-day practices in training camp: I found out that those two-a-days were not bothering me at all. I had never experienced such a thing in all my years of playing football. After one practice session the player in the locker next to mine remarked, "Raymond, your tee shirt is hardly damp." I just hadn't realized what tremendous condition I really was in.

The fact of the matter was that before reporting to camp that year I had not only gone through the "game," doing all the offensive plays, but I had also done the defensive plays as well! Fear can really motivate you if something is very important to you.

I had always hated two-a-day practices because I disliked the physical suffering involved in struggling just to survive. I never went to training camp in the years that followed without working myself into perfect condition *before* reporting. Consequently, this phase of football became a lot easier. I preferred to get my suffering out of the way before I got there. Some of your players might prefer to do the same thing.

There are several reasons and advantages to reporting in *game* condition:

1. A player has the best possible chance of avoiding injury.

2. Athletes can begin immediately to improve their football skills, rather than just trying to survive the physical grind.

3. Players are mentally more alert to what is going on; therefore, they will learn more and get a lot more from the early practices.

4. There's a good chance that the players they are competing against for a position are not in as good condition as an athlete who has made a point of being ready. This can give him an edge.

5. Two-a-days are the toughest part of the football player's year. Being in top condition makes it much easier on him physically and mentally. It makes this part of his season almost bearable.

6. If the athlete does get some kind of injury, he will heal more quickly and he can weather a layoff since he is already in top condition. When he can return he will recover his effectiveness more quickly.

There is a great advantage to utilizing the "playing a game" method of getting your players into condition. This is, *that they know exactly where they are, compared to where they desire to be.* If they go out onto the field with a complete game listed play by play, both the players and you, the coach, know exactly where they decide to quit if they can't go the full game. The next time out, they have a more immediate goal to achieve, going farther on the sheet than they did the previous time. Wherever they stop, they know it. On the other hand, if they do go all the way and complete the game, they know that, too, and the sense of accomplishment they experience going into two-a-days is a valuable, positive boost to their confidence.

An individual conditioning program such as this one should begin about six weeks prior to the opening of drills. That should allow sufficient time for everyone who is using this method to get into reasonable condition.

For players whose game assignments involve a great deal of impact and pushing and driving and hand-to-hand combat—like offensive and defensive linemen—this is not the best type of conditioning test. Neither is it necessarily the best indication of a running back's condition, since it is not an exact duplication of game conditions. However, for receivers it is practically a fool-proof method.

I used several different methods to get into top shape. The first one is the *complete game.* (See Figure 8-1 below for an example.)

Figure 8-1

This is the game our receivers have used to get themselves into condition before reporting. It was an actual game in which the team had to come from behind in the second half.

Procedure: The receiver *sprints* the distance indicated, then he trots back to the "huddle." He pauses 10 to 15 seconds, then returns to the line of scrimmage to run the next play. All assignments are run at full speed for the distance indicated. Between each series, he can take a 3- or 4-minute rest. Then he moves on to the next series and begins. He should take a 15- to 20-minute half time and he should allow a total of two hours to complete.

1st Quarter

(1st Series)   *(2nd Series)*

Sprint 15 yards   Sprint 15 yards

Sprint 15 yards   Sprint 45 yards

Sprint 20 yards   Sprint 15 yards

Sprint 10 yards   Sprint 15 yards

Sprint 10 yards   Sprint 10 yards

Sprint 15 yards

(3rd Series)

Sprint 50 yards

2nd Quarter

(4th Series)   *(5th Series)*

Sprint 20 yards   Sprint 15 yards

Sprint 10 yards   Sprint 30 yards

Sprint 50 yards   Sprint 25 yards

Sprint 10 yards   Sprint 15 yards

Sprint 25 yards   Sprint 15 yards

Sprint 10 yards   *(6th Series)*

Sprint 15 yards   Sprint 30 yards

Sprint 15 yards   Sprint 10 yards

Sprint 5 yards   Sprint 25 yards

Sprint 10 yards   Sprint 20 yards

Sprint 20 yards   Sprint 30 yards

Sprint 35 yards   Sprint 60 yards

Sprint 10 yards   Sprint 20 yards

34 Plays in the 1st Half—21 Runs, 13 Passes.

3rd Quarter

(1st Series)	*(2nd Series)*
Sprint 10 yards	Sprint 10 yards
Sprint 15 yards	Sprint 35 yards
Sprint 25 yards	Sprint 10 yards
Sprint 30 yards	Sprint 15 yards
Sprint 15 yards	Sprint 30 yards
Sprint 20 yards	

(3rd Series)	*(4th Series)*
Sprint 20 yards	Sprint 10 yards
Sprint 10 yards	Sprint 30 yards
Sprint 15 yards	Sprint 20 yards
Sprint 15 yards	Sprint 15 yards
Sprint 25 yards	Sprint 10 yards
Sprint 25 yards	
Sprint 15 yards	

4th Quarter

(5th Series)	*(6th Series)*
Sprint 20 yards	Sprint 35 yards
Sprint 25 yards	Sprint 15 yards
Sprint 65 yards	Sprint 25 yards
Sprint 25 yards	Sprint 35 yards
Sprint 25 yards	Sprint 25 yards
Sprint 30 yards	Sprint 30 yards
Sprint 30 yards	Sprint 30 yards
Sprint 35 yards	
Sprint 50 yards	

40 Plays in the 2nd Half—14 Runs, 26 Passes.

Once I learned *how* to get in shape on my own and *know* it, I used several approaches, not just the *complete game* method. Like most people, I liked a little variety. Jack Patterson, a famed track coach at Baylor University and the University of Texas gave me three endurance builders or endurance testers. (See Figure 8-2 below for examples of all three.)

Figure 8-2

Three methods of building endurance
(use only one of these on any particular day)

1.

Run 150 yards fast. Jog back to the starting point. (No pausing.)
Run 150 yards fast. Jog back. (No pausing.)
Run 150 yards the best you can. Jog back. (No pausing.)
Run 150 yards the best you can. Jog back. (No pausing.)
Run 150 yards the best you can. Jog back. (No pausing.)
Run 150 yards the best you can. Jog back.

2.

Run 330 yards. No pause and jog 110. (No pausing.)
Run 220 yards. No pause and jog 110. (No pausing.)
Run 110 yards.

3.

On a football field, use the back boundary of the end zone for the starting point.
Run 25 yards (to the 15-yard line). Jog back. No pause.
Run 50 yards (to the 40-yard line). Jog back. No pause.
Run 75 yards (to the 35-yard line). Jog back. No pause.
Run 100 yards (to the 10-yard line). Jog back. No pause.
Run 120 yards (to the end line). Jog back. No pause.
Run 120 yards (to the end line). Jog back.

I've used the third method as a conditioning test for the receivers when they report back. The best time made in the first year was 3 minutes and 7 seconds—by a split receiver. The best time the second year was 2 minutes and 45 seconds—by a 220-pound tight end.

A method I used myself during the first two weeks of early conditioning was similar to the method described earlier in the section on increasing speed. This is the use of "accelerations," "build-ups," or "booms" without reaching full speed. The routine was to first warm up and stretch. Next, after I was good and loose, I ran a lot of straightaways, walking the curves on a 440-yard track and then starting at a controlled speed into the straightaway stressing form. I concentrated on pointing my toes straight ahead, getting good knee lift, reaching out with long strides and maintaining a relaxed upper body, while not running flat-footed.

One rule I followed was that I avoided full speed sprinting and starts and really quick movements for the first two weeks of conditioning. This was because normally I was coming off of a three-month layoff—January, February, and March. The object was to get the muscles back in tone gradually, thus avoiding muscle pulls or strains.

After a couple of weeks I started increasing the tempo and the speed. Once I felt my legs were ready for full speed work, I started running more pass routes. Running moves are one of the most demanding things a receiver can do as far as his legs are concerned. Running 30 to 40 routes at full speed is a good conditioner.

The other great conditioner I used is described in detail in Chapter Six, "Running with the Football." This chapter involves working with diagrams of good runners and the maneuvers they have used to elude tacklers and regain their balance. I had 15 to 20 "runs," which I would re-enact in their entirety at full speed. By having a variety of conditioning drills at my disposal, I avoided becoming bored with getting into shape. Using "Running with the Football" and

"Moves" as a conditioner allows you to combine conditioning with developing football skills.

THE SECOND GOAL—MAXIMUM SPRING, BOUNCE, AND ZIP ON GAME DAY

This subject is one which I paid a high price to learn. I made some big mistakes in this area. I'm sure it may vary for different athletes, but in coaching I've found that one thing doesn't vary: What I learned the hard way is that there are some physical laws that you don't break—they break you.

For example, a baseball pitcher knows that if he pitches nine innings he had better wait three days before pitching again. He can violate this law if he chooses to, but if he does, sooner or later he will pay the price with his arm.

I had a tendency to work too hard, to run too much. What I didn't realize at first was that there are *Two Phases* to conditioning:

1. What an athlete does to get into top shape.
2. What an athlete does *after* he gets into top shape to maintain it.

Once an athlete gets into top shape he doesn't have to maintain the same amount of work to stay in shape. If he does overwork *after* getting into shape, his performance will really suffer and he will be a more likely candidate for a muscle pull.

Bob Shaw joined the Colts Coaching Staff after my third year in Baltimore. He was an ex-pro receiver who had once scored five touchdowns in a single game, and had played with the Cardinals and the Rams. He watched me working in practice and during two-a-days he told me, "Raymond, you're doing too much running." Bob Shaw kept after me all year and gradually, he began to reach me. My dad had been telling me pretty much the same thing for years: that once you reach top condition, you don't work as hard.

The next year, my fifth in pro ball, I finally started cutting back on the amount of running I was doing in practice. This was, of course, after the season began. For the first time in my pro career I discovered what it was like to have a lot of spring, bounce, and zip in my legs on game day!

Bob left the Colts and I began to revert back to my old ways. The next year I got carried away during the season and was sprinting all over the field during practice and then running routes after practice. Right during the middle of the season, the law caught up with me. Enroute to Chicago to play the Bears I noticed that my hamstring muscle in my right leg was twitching periodically. I didn't realize then what it was telling me. The next day, early in the second quarter, I felt a severe pain in the back of my leg. I had pushed it too far, and for the next two weeks I was out of action.

So don't let your receivers leave their games on the practice field. A young athlete trying to make the team or please the coach may not have the experience or the confidence not to overwork. Plan the week so that your players are raring to go on game day. The receiver will get open and catch the ball at his best if his legs are feeling good.

One rule of thumb I learned is that a total of 40 pass routes in any one practice session is enough. Put a check on your players to see that they don't exceed this number. This rule of thumb refers to early in the practice week. Two days before the game, 15 pass routes is plenty.

THE THIRD GOAL—
MINIMUM LOSS OF PRACTICE TIME,
GAME TIME, DUE TO INJURIES

One of the biggest wastes to the athlete comes from losing time on the practice field and in games due to injuries that could have been prevented. There are a lot of things players *can* do and a lot of things they *should not* do in order to maximize their playing time. As coaches, most of us know pretty well what is safe to do and what isn't. But often, players will not think ahead to the consequences of some of the things they attempt. Often, we need to inform them what may happen if they are careless or reckless in regard to their physical fitness and safety.

I learned early the painful lesson that *injuries can cost you.* As a sophomore and also as a junior in college I had a groin pull that caused me to miss the first part of our practices—two weeks. This was due to my ignorance of how to prepare myself physically *before* reporting for two-a-days. It cost me a chance to make the team. So I began to observe all I could, and also to learn from personal experiences. It became engrained in me, over the years, which things to do and which things not to do. I learned to be on my guard constantly and to play the odds. The object was to develop good judgment about a variety of things so I could be on that practice field and ready to go for games. This is absolutely essential if an athlete hopes to develop and reach his full potential. I made some big mistakes and I saw some others do the same. Maybe you can use some of these experiences to help educate your athletes so that they will not have to go over the same ground I already covered.

Strength Building: I was really bothered by finger and thumb sprains for a long time. Then our trainer got some putty to work with. After learning how to use it I had very, very few finger and thumb injuries. Then when I did get one, it healed very quickly and the loss of time was cut to a day or two. Basically, this is the same principle applied to other joints and parts of the body. If you can put the athlete on the right program to build the area he needs built up, do it. Then when that particular part of his body gets "tested" by a blow, it is prepared and has a maximum chance of standing the shock. I used to work nine months of the year on developing strength in my neck, shoulders, arms, upper body, stomach, low back, and legs. There are many different ways to do this by using exercises or weights or a combination of both.

Preventing Muscle Pulls: I try to teach and warn my receivers about the danger signals muscles give—tightening up, aching, slight throbbing, etc. I insist that they tell me the instant they get a warning light. The best way to treat a muscle like that is to quit right then. In practically every case, he will miss only one day. Once he pulls a muscle, however, it takes anywhere from a week to two weeks to heal properly. Prevention is the best approach.

Other mistakes to warn your athletes to avoid:

- Failure to warm up properly and stretch and loosen up before going full speed in starts or sprints.
- Running too much or too fast when they have not adequately rested. A fatigued muscle is a prime candidate for a pull.
- Doing too much speed work when the legs are not in good condition or when they are tight or very tired.
- Failure to replace body salts and fluids lost through heavy sweating. There are several good commercial drinks to aid in overcoming this problem. I like my receivers to use them during the game and during practice.

Knowing When to Quit: The wide receiver position is the pro-type offense that requires a tremendous amount of full speed running. I believe *every* assignment is important, pass or run, and that there is no time to be saving yourself during a game. I know from personal experience and from coaching that on game day an athlete *can* play with this type of effort.

During the off-season when players are working out, and during the season, as they prepare week by week, they need to have a good grasp of *when to quit, when they've done enough, when it's time to call a halt.*

A primary point to think about during the season is to *be ready for the game, be at maximum freshness, with maximum spring and bounce.* They should not leave the game on the practice field. The tendency is to run receivers too much, without realizing how much they have done.

Some questions to ask are: Do the receivers have dead legs? Do they feel fresh and raring to go the night of the game? How much practice time and game time are we losing due to injuries? Are we getting muscle pulls? Are we losing players in practices or in games? How many routes are our receivers running per day? How many running plays? Would we be better off to limit practices more than we do now?

One year in late November I sprained my ankle slightly in a game and was forced to lay off three or four days completely. I took part in the final practice and was ready to go for the next game. I couldn't believe the difference in my legs! I had more spring, speed, quickness, and agility than I'd had in weeks. As the season had gone on, what had happened was that gradually my legs had been drained, but I hadn't realized it. That three or four days off made a *big* difference. My performance benefited as well.

Your players have got to know when to quit in the off-season, too. I don't think a youngster should ever work more than an hour in the off-season. I'm talking about a player who is out there working and not just socializing. My dad gave me a rule of thumb I finally learned after about five or six years of overdoing it. He told me, "If you will always quit while you are still feeling good, you will always feel good the next workout." He was right. In my earlier years I ran way too much. Later when I learned how to, I never worked longer than an hour, usually 45 minutes. I never did more than four or five days a week, either.

A young player, experienced or not, can easily overdo. In his eagerness to please the coach, or to make the team, or to keep up with other players as he feels he should, it can be easy to overwork. There is a certain amount of pain and suffering involved in getting into good shape. That, however, should not be the overwhelming sensation or the gauge of progress. It is not true that the more pain an athlete feels the better shape he is getting into or even the faster progress he is making.

Especially during the off-season or pre-season, we should try to insure that the players are not faced with too much drudgery or boredom. Players can utilize a variety of drills, exercises, and activities to achieve good conditioning. Some of these activities can even be fun. A little fun and a little variety can make practice almost fun. Mental fatigue can be just as damaging to the athlete as physical fatigue. We need to encourage our players to get into shape slowly, without burning themselves out or losing interest or sight of the season ahead of them.

As bodies get into condition, there can be advantages to friendly games and competition within the squad. Such activities can inject interest into what is being accomplished. As athletes get into shape they can receive additional motivation from competing with teammates and finding pleasure in running faster than someone who was faster the year before. Sometimes an athlete will try a little harder in a game than when taking part in a drill. In either case they can see that they are making progress.

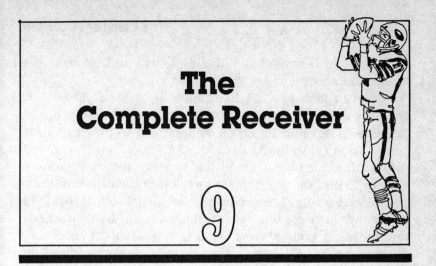

The Complete Receiver

9

THE COMPLETE RECEIVER—MENTALLY

Striving to Win

All of us desire to play on a winning team. Nothing can substitute for that goal. Neither can anyone *guarantee* victory. We must turn our attention to doing those things that will give us the best chance of reaching our full potential. The individual player must focus his concentration on the things he has control over; the things that will result in his making his best contribution. He must realize that each play, each assignment, can mean the championship.

During the course of a game a player never knows ahead of time which play may be the turning point of a game—the key play that opens the way to victory. Consequently, he should train himself to give *maximum effort and concentration* to one play at a time. He can't look back; he can't look ahead; he must carry out his assignment *now*. This results in a consistent performance. It means he will not allow an early failure to bother him. It also means some early success (a big play) will not satisfy him.

In pressure situations he wants the pass thrown to him; he wants the play run behind his block. When the outcome of the play can mean victory or defeat, he wants to be in the middle of it. He welcomes the challenge and believes his maximum effort will be equal to the challenge.

Eleven men playing like this will be tough to beat. It requires great physical condition and mental discipline in practice to develop this type of approach to playing. Your players don't save themselves for anything. They put all-out effort into each play. This will give them the best possible chance to become winners, to develop to the fullest of their potential. You don't have control over all the factors that lead to championships, but you do have control over practices and teaching your players what is important in becoming champions. Your players have control over their individual effort.

Being Coachable

All coaches desire to work with athletes who are coachable and willing to work. Being such an athlete reflects an attitude. Attitudes can be altered. They are the result of habits of thinking. By reinforcing the kind of behavior we wish our players to exhibit, we encourage them to act in acceptable ways. When they begin to act in the manner we want, they are changing their habits of thinking and this will result in changes of attitude. Such changes will be encouraged quicker if they are met with words of encouragement and praise.

In becoming coachable, players learn what is important to the coach and they act and react to conform to the standards of the coach. If we can field eleven players who are striving to meet the same standards and are willingly conforming to what the coach wants, then the team truly reflects the coach.

The Importance of Little Things

How much of a margin separates the winner from the loser when two evenly matched teams confront each other?

A motion penalty nullifies a long run from scrimmage. The loss is not just the 5 yards penalized, but the long gain resulting from the run, good field position, a possible scoring opportunity, and a blow to morale and confidence. . . . A sideline pass barely misfires as the receiver fails to keep his feet in bounds as he makes the catch. The loss is a first down, loss of possession, loss of precious time as his team is desperately trying to come from behind in the 4th quarter.

In your preparations and practices your players never know which detail they are working on will be the one that wins a game for you. Every practice, every meeting is important. Especially when your opponent is your equal or better, it is necessary to gain an edge somewhere—by hustling, a fumble recovery, a key block. The complete receiver knows that that is no such thing as a *little* detail if it can win a game for you.

If a team puts forth its best effort and falls short, that's one thing. But if players are careless and cost the team, that is entirely different.

Building Confidence—Dealing with Fear

I had two distinct experiences regarding confidence and fear that have left a lasting impression on me. I know personally that fear and lack of confidence can paralyze one's physical abilities. It is not a pleasant experience. While playing football at SMU during my college days I completely lost my confidence in my speed. Coaches and other people had been telling me long enough that I was slow and I finally got to believing it, too. I'll never forget lining up at defensive end and watching a sweep come my way. My mind was in such a negative state that I could hardly move. It wasn't until a year or two later that this damaging image of myself was corrected. I'll always remember the feeling I got when after working out with the track team for awhile I found I could run with the sprinters after learning the proper form and techniques. The point here is that my mental state changed from a negative one concerning my ability to a positive one. Once I discovered that I was not slow, it was never a problem again.

The second experience happened my second year in pro ball. I was under a tremendous amount of pressure. I was very afraid of getting cut. The demands of management, my teammates, my coaches and myself were pressing in on me and it was more than I could handle. Knowing the slightest mistake could put me on the road, I began to doubt my overall ability. I had always had a lot of confidence in my ability to catch a football, but suddenly I found myself without this confidence. In our opening pre-season game with the Eagles I broke open on a Deep Post route. As the ball floated down, my thoughts said to me, "You're going to drop it. You're going to drop it." I did. For the next several weeks I hoped desperately that the quarterback would not throw the ball to me. I had completely lost my confidence.

Perhaps you have never had experiences like these. If so, be thankful. If you have been through something similar, you know what I'm talking about.

I've learned two things about acquiring and developing and maintaining confidence. First, I must personally go along with David, the great Biblical personality who stated in the Psalms: "The Lord is my confidence." This is in the spiritual realm. Second, in the physical realm, I believe proper training and preparation can greatly increase your chances for success, and I believe success leads to confidence.

I know that by proper training and repetition of running in track my speed potential developed and vastly improved. This led to faster starts and the ability to compete with sprinters in good enough fashion that I experienced success in races. This led to confidence.

I know that the proper training program in catching can take a boy's ability and help him develop and improve it vastly. This was my experience and the payoff comes in making catches you could not otherwise make. Again, success in catching leads to confidence. Confidence then leads to better performance.

I think with young players who are trying to prove themselves, it is especially important to have a sound foundation of proper training, repetition, and practice. You want these types of players in situations where they have the best possible chances of being successful. In the formative stages they can go either up or down very quickly.

Here is a statement I read once and believe to be true: "Confidence is the end product of a mastered skill."

A Game of Inches

It was a crucial Baltimore-Green Bay Packer game. The Western Division Title was riding on the outcome. It was 3rd and 6, the Colts had the ball inside the Packer 30-yard line, threatening and needing one touchdown to go ahead late in the 4th quarter. Willie Davis, the great Packer defensive end was fighting to get to Unitas in an effort to force an incompletion. A Colt receiver broke open over the middle with clear sailing to the goal line. Davis was closing in on Unitas with great effort. Unitas released the ball, but just as he did Willie Davis managed to barely get a piece of the ball. It wasn't very much, but it took some of the trajectory off of the throw. The receiver had to slow down slightly and reach down for a low pass. This delay turned a potential touchdown into a 20-yard gain and a 1st down. On the next play, the Colts fumbled, the Packers recovered, and then ran out the clock. If Willie Davis had been just a few inches later, Baltimore would have won. It's a game of inches. A little extra strength, a little extra endurance, a little extra determination—somewhere along the line the great Packer defensive end paid a price. The payoff was mighty big as they went on to a Championship.

Bill McClard of the University of Arkansas put his foot into the ball in a field goal attempt of 60 yards against SMU. The ball floated down and *hit the crossbar*, bounced high in the air, and dropped over. It was good—a new NCAA record. The thing I had to contemplate is the effort and work Bill had put into kicking for over five years; the disciplined program of exercise and weight lifting he had used to develop strength in his legs; the way he had worked in the summer on a daily kicking routine. I thought to myself, "Somewhere along the line he picked up strength and accuracy in an extra amount, enough to give him an extra inch or two. And that extra inch or two was precisely the difference on that kick. Two inches less and it would not have been good."

In any area of football you care to examine, you can see very dramatically that football is a game of inches. A receiver gets to a pass by inches; a defender leaps to intercept or deflect a pass and makes it by inches; a lineman makes a last gasp effort and keeps his man off of the passer by inches.

To the individual athlete this means that if his extra work and effort pays off in increasing his speed by inches, it can mean the difference. If it pays off in increasing his strength, or whatever the area in which he's working—just a slight margin can mean the difference between success and failure.

Building Team Unity and Spirit

Building team unity and spirit is an absolute necessity if you are going to have a championship team, in my opinion. The first priority has to be on *winning*. Second, the natural tendency to think about ourselves first that we all have must be recognized, and then squelched as much as is humanly possible. That doesn't mean we can't have a desire to excel at our position, but it does mean the interests of the team come first.

On offense, this means the attitude that we don't care how we're moving the ball or who is doing it. Our objective is to move the ball and score with it. Don't care how or who as long as the job is being done. On defense, it means not being concerned with who's making the tackles; rather, one should be concerned with stopping the opponent as long as they're stopped.

The complete player will encourage his teammates when they make a mistake. He will congratulate them when they make a good play. When a player makes a mistake himself, he will not make excuses or try to shift the blame. He will make his contribution, whatever it may be. Everyone can contribute something—the attitude, effort, and enthusiasm can inspire others. It rubs off. Griping and complaining should be avoided at all costs. They tear down team unity.

Dealing with Adversity

An athlete comes up against a variety of trials, tests, defeats, adversity. Losing a game can result in a tendency to panic, to feel sorry for oneself, to blame others, to blow up. This must be recognized and avoided at all costs.

The number one question to answer is this: is the effort there? Have we been doing all we can? We always hope it will be enough. If it isn't, we have done all we could. We can't let one defeat lead to another.

Time and time again we hear about teams or individuals who have turned adversity into opportunity, into stepping stones to higher achievements. I think the key thing is how our athletes react to setbacks or trials. They can either go forward or backward.

Drop a Pass?

It's possible for a receiver to let a dropped pass early in the game cause him to perform poorly from then on. I learned this the hard way while playing in junior college. I dropped a pass that would have been a long gainer. Brooding and worrying about it, I played poorly the rest of the game. At that time I didn't know anything about how to develop catching ability. Later, however, as coach of college receivers at the University of Arkansas, this is the approach I took: We had a practice routine that we stuck to day after day, week after week. The players worked in a disciplined manner trying to master the 15-20 types of catches that exist. If we missed one in a game, there was nothing more that could have been done, so we didn't sweat it. I told them to analyze a drop to see what caused it so we could work on it the next week, then we would forget it and think about making the next catch, which might win the game for us. Of course, if a receiver hasn't really worked and prepared himself and he drops one, there's no one to blame but himself.

As a player it really teed me off to miss a pass. However, working and preparing for a pass helped me mentally; just knowing I'd done all I could was a big comfort. I couldn't have lived with myself if carelessness had led to dropping a pass.

If someone asks a complete receiver who drops a pass, "What happened?" he will tell them, "I missed it." He won't come off the field or back to the huddle with his head down.

The complete receiver must be as tough mentally as he is expected to be physically. He needs to maintain control of his emotions. He cannot afford to lose his concentration during a game. He has to keep his composure and control.

What Is a Competitor?

- He plays every play like it means the championship.
- He never gives up; he is never beat mentally.
- He's a game player. He comes through when his team needs it most.
- He is consistent. He does his job play after play.
- He makes tough catches. You can't knock him loose from the ball.
- Dropping a pass doesn't discourage him. He comes right back and gets the next one.
- He pursues and tackles when there is an interception.
- He's not satisfied with his performance.
- He keeps going when he's tired.
- He comes off the line on every play like he is the number one receiver, even on running plays. He runs the defender to death. A defensive back can't relax for a moment.
- He doesn't play cautiously. He's aggressive and always on the attack.
- He's more interested in winning than anything else.

PHYSICALLY

Reports in Condition

When the complete receiver reports for practice the first day, he is in condition. He knows the importance of starting in shape. He avoids the agony of getting into condition during two-a-days, which allows him to concentrate on learning his assignments and perfecting his techniques. He will not suffer from chronic injuries and even when he is injured, he will recover with greater speed.

Practices 100%

The minute he steps onto the practice field he is all business. He works hard to strengthen any weaknesses he may have in an attempt to convert them into strengths. The complete receiver works hard on his blocking and takes pride in being a consistent and effective blocker. He puts the same effort into all aspects of his game. He leads by example and constantly strives to reach his full potential.

Runs Exact Disciplined Routes

The complete receiver strives to execute all of his patterns with equal success. He runs his routes in practice just as he does in the games. The quarterback knows when and where the break will be made. Each receiver knows the routes of the other receivers and makes sure he runs his routes to facilitate the coordination of the full pattern.

Has Highly Developed Catching Skills

In order for every receiver to be a complete receiver, he must be able to catch the football—consistently, regardless of where the pass is thrown. If he has worked hard to develop his catching skills by working on the mastery of the types of catches, he will catch most balls thrown to him that he gets his hands on. Like every skill, mastery comes only through correct repetition. No phase of the pass-catching art can be slighted. If the receiver has a weakness in any area, he must practice harder to make up for the deficiency and convert it into a strength.

Mastery of the pass-catching skills is like conditioning. Neither of these areas is a three- or four-month-out-of-the-year process. To review their skills, receivers must work before the season starts. No receiver should ever be satisfied with his proficiency. He should always be striving to improve in some area.

Can Run with the Ball After the Catch

When the opportunity presents itself, the complete receiver can run with the ball to advance it toward the goal while maintaining possession. This ability is also a developed skill, an area of the game he has prepared for by thinking about and practicing.

The coaching adage that success occurs when preparation meets with opportunity is very true. The receivers who run successfully after they have caught a pass are the ones who have practiced doing just that. Very few good things just happen in football. Successful receivers are like successful coaches, they have a plan for every situation. They have practiced it and they have confidence that it will work.

Doesn't Fumble

A fumble in almost every instance is a mistake that results from carelessness or a lack of concentration. Complete receivers automatically tuck the ball securely away after every catch. This is the result of doing just that after every catch in practice and drills. The act of tucking the ball away is an integral part of the catch itself and the complete receiver knows that. For this action to become automatic, the receiver needs to concentrate on it everytime he catches a football.

Blocks with Effort

The average practice for many receivers has them running pass patterns and working on catching drills. Consequently, they often spend little time on perfecting their blocking ability. If the primary purpose of the receiver in an offense is to get himself open and catch the ball, then he needs to spend the majority of his time on those areas of his game. Even in such a situation, he will have to block effectively. Although he may not be as skilled a blocker as he is a receiver, he should know his assignments perfectly and can help offset his lack of skill with an extra amount of effort whenever he is called upon to block. Such effort needs to be practiced to be consistent. While he may not be as skilled a blocker, there is no excuse for him not to be effective.

Plays Aggressively

While aggressiveness is in one respect a mental characteristic, it can be very physical. The complete receiver is aggressive when he goes after any pass thrown in his area. He must have every intention of catching it, despite any obstacle. An aggressive receiver blocks with authority and does not let up or take it easy because the play is designed to go the other way. When he is supposed to be in a certain position to block a defender, he not only is there at the right time, but is there with a hard, aggressive block that guarantees that the defender will not recover sufficiently enough to get in on the play. He demonstrates his aggressiveness by being around the action and being actively involved in any way that can contribute to his team's effort.

Exhibits Pride

Pride is another aspect of the receiver primarily thought of as a mental aspect. Physically, the receiver exhibits his pride by his appearance, his performance, and his willingness to accept leadership. His equipment is never abused, his uniform is reasonably clean, and he takes pride in looking good and playing well. He always gives all his effort in practice and in games, regardless of the score. He takes pride in doing his best; he wants others to see that he is performing at his best. He welcomes his role of leading by example—of doing his best all the time, and by doing so, encouraging his teammates to do the same. By doing this, he encourages the pride of several individuals to become a team pride.

Index